ACKNOWLEDGMENTS

To my children, Gretchen and Jesse, and to our friend Sherie, many thanks for putting up with me during the writing of this book.

I'd also like to thank my writing buddies, Kathy Deady, Muriel Dubois, Jennifer Ericsson, Andrea Murphy, Barbara Turner, and Sally Wilkins, as well as my Billerica group, Diane Davis, Peter Davis, and Marion Eldridge. Anyone who writes and has a good critique group knows that the support of the group is invaluable. I'm lucky enough to have two great groups!

A special thank you to Diane Davis who read and commented on most of the manuscript. Diane is always full of wonderful ideas! Thanks to my other readers, Norm Clairmont, Tom Corvi, and John Freeston.

I need to acknowledge the support of my coworkers at the Nesmith Library in Windham, NH, and give a special thanks to Joe Mayr who loaned me his library card so that I could also "raid" the libraries of Massachusetts.

The Internet and e-mail has made research materials more accessible. It has also allowed me to "interview" kids for the project. Therefore, I'd like to give a great big thank you to my writing buddies and the people on the Children's Writers and CHILIS listservs who connected me with their kids. Rosemary E., Monica and Natalie N., Justin W., Joanne B., Ryan K., James M., Valerie L., Austin P., Tyler S., Matthew R., Ashley S., Lynn B., Becki D., April G., DJ, LaTroi and Kyler W., Dominika R., and Ryan, your answers to my questions were a BIG help.

To Susan Smulski of BankBoston's Salem, NH branch, who was kind enough to take time to answer my questions, thank you.

I apologize to anyone whose name has been omitted. It's not that I don't appreciate your help, it's just that my organizational skills leave a lot to be desired!

CONTENTS

CONTENTS

INTRODUCTION

Everything a kid should know about money? That's a tall order! Since every kid is different, I thought I'd ask a few what they would like to know about money.

- James M. of Sound Beach, New York, wanted to find out how an ATM works.
- Natalie N. of Ambler, Pennsylvania asked, "When was the first dollar bill made?"
- Natalie's sister Monica was interested in learning about banking accounts and checks.
- Tyler S., Mountain Ranch, California said, "I would like to know if kids can invest in the stock market and how to do it."
- From Chelmsford, Massachusetts, came Joanne B.'s question, "How much does the government make a day?"*
- Here's one from Justin W. of Marshall, Michigan: "How come things cost more today than when my mom and dad were kids?"
- Chelsea D. of Birmingham, Alabama asked what I'm sure most kids would like to know, "How do I make a lot of money fast?"

So many good questions! In the chapters that follow I'm going to try to answer these, and more, of the questions you may have about money.

---

* Here's a partial answer to Joanne B.'s question. The U.S. government estimates that it will make $1.794 trillion in the year 2000. To figure out how much that is a day, divide by 365! (I hope Joanne has a calculator! Trying to figure out how many zeros there are in a trillion gives me a headache!)

The answer is $4.915 billion a day.

Chapter 1
What Is Money?

A PENNY'S WORTH OF MONEY HISTORY

BARTER

If you've ever traded the banana from your lunch for someone else's snackpack of potato chips, then you've taken part in one of the oldest forms of buying and selling—barter.

Bartering works fairly well as long as the goods being exchanged have the same **value**, like the chips and the banana. But, what if you wanted to trade a bicycle? How many bags of chips would equal one bicycle? Probably too many for you to think about without feeling queasy!

Thousands of years ago people traded with each other on a small scale—one farmer's grapes for another's pumpkins. This worked for a while, but as life became more complex so did the system of bartering. Some people did not farm. They developed other skills such as tool making or basket weaving.

A basketmaker may want to buy some grapes, but the farmer already has enough baskets and won't make a trade. A toolmaker needs a basket, so he asks the basketmaker to trade for a knife. The basket maker now has a knife that he takes to the farmer to see if the farmer will

> "Money does not occur in nature, and no version or analog of it exists among any members of the animal kingdom. Money, like language, is uniquely human."
> —*Jack Weatherford*

WORDS to KNOW

Value—the worth of an object

Commodity—any good that is used in trade. In the past commodities were primarily agricultural products. Even today, commodities such as sugar, coffee, wheat, soybeans, and cattle are traded on commodity exchanges. Other commodities such as silver and gold, oil, and foreign currencies are also traded.

FUN FACT

In Europe, after World War II, an unofficial form of commodity money was popular—chocolate bars! The chocolate was brought to the area by American soldiers who were there to help rebuild war-torn Europe.

accept it in exchange for grapes. He will, and the trade is made—but what an uncertain business it is! The poor basketmaker could have just as easily ended up grapeless! And what if the basketmaker needed only a few grapes for his lunch? Could the knife have been divided up into smaller pieces? Not if it was to retain its value!

COMMODITIES

A better way of doing business was needed. Commodity money! Barley is an example of a grain that was used for trade. It was accepted by the traders as payment. The basketmaker would take barley as payment for a basket. The farmer would take the basketmaker's barley for grapes. The toolmaker would take the farmer's barley in trade for a knife. The basketmaker could buy a handful of grapes for a small measure of barley. Business could be done more efficiently.

Barley also had its problems. It could spoil or become infested with bugs. If one year a barley harvest was poor, then there would be very little to use in trade. And there was the problem of transporting it! Another change was needed. Perishable money was replaced by a harder form of money.

QUIZ

Here are five examples of commodity money that have been traded in the past. Match them up with the country or area where they were popular.

Commodity

1. Rice
2. Cacao beans (chocolate)
3. Reindeer
4. Dried codfish
5. Cattle

Area

A. Norway
B. Siberia
C. Southern Africa
D. Japan
E. Mexico

Answers: 1(D); 2(E); 3(B); 4(A); 5(C)

FUN FACT

Cowrie shells were so widely used as currency that when it came time to choose a scientific name for the cowrie, the name chosen was *Cuprea moneta*, "money cowries." Cowrie shells were still being used for trade in rural parts of Nigeria as late as 1935!

$ $ $

Counterfeiting is not just a modern problem—in colonial times, counterfeiters dyed white beads black!

Although never a preferred form of currency, wampum was useful for many years. A factory opened in New Jersey in 1760 and began to **mass produce** wampum beads. The value of wampum fell. It was no longer accepted as money.

$ $ $

In early America nails were made one by one by blacksmiths and thus were expensive. Old homes were burned down so that the nails could be recovered and used again! Like wampum, the value of nails dropped when factories began to mass produce them.

CURRENCY

The invention of hard money required a considerable amount of trust. Trust in one's fellow traders to come to an agreement on the value to be placed on the token chosen to be used in trade.

If all the people in a village decide that five blue pebbles is equal to one chicken, and thirty blue pebbles is equal to one goat, then an active trade can be set up using blue pebbles as money. Based upon the price of a chicken, the villagers decide that a bowl of corn is worth one pebble.

As long as all the parties involved agree, then the village can have a blue pebble **currency**. The blue pebbles are chosen because of their beauty and rarity. Blue pebbles are found only at the back of a deep, dark, scary cave fifty miles away in the mountains. If the villagers had chosen white pebbles, they wouldn't have worked as currency because white pebbles are found everywhere in the village. They have no value.

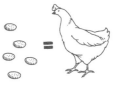

Shell Money

Cowrie shells were used as money in China at least as far back as 3,500 years ago. As a matter of fact, the

WORDS to KNOW

Currency—money in any form that is actively used in trade.

It is not known what the first currency was, but from hieroglyphics found in the Middle East, we do know that currency in one form or another has been in existence for thousands of years. It is believed that writing first came about as a way of keeping **accounts**!

Accounts—records of business transactions.

Shell It Out

The next time you hear someone complain, "I had to shell out" think about how much more he or she would have to complain about if they really had to "shell out" shells!

WORDS to KNOW

Legal tender—the money that a government says is acceptable as payment for debts.

Mass produce—to make in large quantities.

Chinese character for money was based on the cowrie shell.

Another form of shell currency, used by Native Americans and early colonists, was wampum. Wampum is beads made of purple (some of them were so dark they were referred to as black) and white seashells strung together to form belts and other objects.

Shells were plentiful along the Atlantic coast, but the amount of time spent making shells into beads was great. The wampum had value because it was beautiful and it required many hours of labor to produce. Purple wampum was more valuable than the white because the purple shells were harder to find, and more difficult to make into beads.

In 1620, the Dutch used wampum in trade with the native peoples of New Amsterdam (now known as New York). By 1627, they had introduced wampum to the Pilgrims of Plymouth, Massachusetts, who traded it for furs. And, fourteen years later, Massachusetts made wampum **legal tender** for small transactions. The exchange rate was set as three purple beads or six white beads being equal to one penny. Later, in New Amsterdam in 1664, wampum was used to pay the wages of

"Wampum" comes from the Algonquin language, *wab* = white, *umpe* = string.

WORD origin

FUN FACT

Strange Money

Over the years, many strange and wonderful things have been used as money—feathers, ivory, shells, salt. In fact, the word salary comes from the Latin word *salarius*, meaning salt. Roman soldiers were paid "salt money," salarium! In the time before refrigerators, salt was needed to keep food from spoiling.

Stone Money

The largest form of money is the giant stone circles used on the Pacific island, Yap. Yap stone money, known as fei stones, come in sizes up to 12 feet across. The largest ones were used as an indication of their owners' wealth. Smaller stone money was used for everyday transactions. For the people of Yap, the money had value because it had come from great distances across the ocean. Carrying it to the island involved much risk!

$ $ $

Wampum wasn't the only substitute for coins in the colonies. In 1619, Virginia declared tobacco to be its official currency. When Sir Walter Raleigh introduced tobacco into England, Queen Elizabeth I is reported to have said, "I have known many persons who turned their gold into smoke, but you are the first to turn smoke into gold."

the workers who built the citadel (a fortress). Shell money was not just for small trades!

Metal Money—Coins

Precious metals such as gold and silver came to be widely accepted as valuable. It wasn't long before people found a way to make it into money!

Metal money has several advantages over the other forms of money discussed so far:

1. The metals used are scarce and thus valuable.
2. It is portable—think about how much easier it is to carry several pieces of gold in your pocket than it is to carry belts of wampum!
3. Its value is accepted in many countries.
4. It is malleable (able to be shaped) and can be divided into little pieces for smaller payments.
5. It's beautiful!

Little bean-like lumps of electrum, a gold-silver mixture found in the riverbeds of Lydia, (an ancient country in the area that is now Turkey) were the first coins that we know of. Around 630 B.C., the king of Lydia had the lumps stamped with a design of the head of a lion, and coins began to be exchanged for goods in Lydia's markets. The Lydians' coins were so well suited as money, the Greeks and the Romans took to **minting** coins of their own.

Metal money was originally traded in lumps, rods, or bars. Its value was in its

WORDS to KNOW

Minting—
the process of stamping pieces of metal to be used as money.

FUN FACT

Hoot Loot!

In Athens, Greece, silver coins called drachmas were imprinted with an owl. These coins were so successful, they continued to be produced for almost six hundred years!

Manillas

In the early 1500s, Portugal sent large quantities of copper and brass to West Africa. Instead of being made into coins, these metals were made into *manillas*. Manilla is the Portuguese word for bracelet. Manillas were worn as bracelets, anklets, and necklaces. They were an easy way to carry money, and the copper and brass were often melted down to make beads and other decorative items.

The Dollar Is Born

In Joachimsthal, Bohemia (in the region that is now the Czech Republic) in 1519, a silver coin was minted. It became known as a *Joachimsthaler*, later shortened to *thaler*. From thaler came the name "dollar" which was also used for the Spanish eight-*reales* piece. This coin, also known as a "piece-of-eight," was so well-known in the United States that when the U.S. government started its own system of money in the late 1700s, it chose the name dollar for its basic unit.

weight. A bigger (heavier) lump was worth more than a small one. Each time a trade was made, the gold or silver had to be weighed to determine its exact value.

As you can imagine, merchants got tired of doing all that weighing! The solution came when merchants began to mark the weight directly on the lump itself.

In the early days of coins, with gold and silver being such soft metals, a dishonest person was able shave off small pieces of the edge of a coin. This was called "clipping." After a while the dishonest person would have a collection of clipped pieces large enough to be melted down and sold. If you look at today's quarter, you will notice ridges around the edge. The ridges are known as reeding or milling. Ridges prevented the clipping of coins. If someone tried to clip off a piece of a reeded edge it would be noticed!

So, now the world had coins, and they worked well, but they were inconvenient for making big payments. Imagine having to carry large amounts of coins over great distances. You would need pack animals. You would be an easy target for thieves. Once again, there needed to be a change in currency—paper money.

Money Clip

An English coin from the first half of the seventeenth century had this message imprinted on the edge: "The penalty for clipping this coin is death."

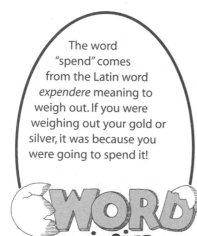

WORD origin

The word "spend" comes from the Latin word *expendere* meaning to weigh out. If you were weighing out your gold or silver, it was because you were going to spend it!

FUN FACT

Stamping Coins

The first coins were minted by hand. A lump of precious metal was put on an anvil; then a stamp-like device was hit with a hammer. The stamp left an impression in the metal.

The quality of coins improved over the years. The lumps were stamped or pressed into more coin-like shapes. They were mostly round, but some had holes in the middle, others were square-shaped, and in 1665, a British brass penny was heart-shaped! The coins were decorated with images of kings, animals, plants, and so on. Words and numbers were also eventually added

Milled Money

In Leonardo da Vinci's notebooks there are drawings for a coin press powered by a water mill. The press produced more uniform coins, something that was difficult to do with the hand method of stamping. Coins made with this press were known as milled money. The process of milling also enabled mints to add reeding to the edges of coins.

Furry Commodity

Skins and furs were used as a form of commodity money in many places. In Russia, some of its first coins were given the names of the skins that had been traded earlier—for example, belka means squirrel, and shkura means hide.

Cash and Carry

Chinese cash were round coins with square holes in the middle. The holes were used to string the coins together to make them easier to carry. Cash was used in China up until the second half of the nineteenth century.

Marco Polo, the great explorer from Venice, Italy, visited China in 1271. There he discovered that the Chinese used paper money. He described it in his journals: "All these pieces of paper are issued with as much solemnity and authority as if they were of pure gold or silver …"

Paper Money

The Chinese are given credit for inventing paper money. Around 86 B.C., Emperor Wu of China used squares of white deerskin, approximately one foot square, for money. These squares of deerskin were decorated around the edges with designs of plants. The Emperor decided that each skin would be equal to four hundred thousand copper coins. Although this money was not used outside the court of the emperor, it is considered a forerunner of paper money.

It wasn't until approximately eight centuries later that money made of real paper was issued in China. It was not like the bills of today. Rather, it was more like today's checks. Merchants put heavy copper coins called *cash*, in the government treasury and were given "certificates of indebtedness" in exchange. Like our modern day checks, these pieces of paper represented the money that was waiting in the treasury. This check-like money was known as *fei-ch'ien*, "flying money." Flying, perhaps, because unlike copper it did not weigh the merchant down!

Paper itself was relatively new to Europeans. The Chinese had discovered how to make paper many hundreds of years before the first paper mill in

Buckskin

A "buck" is slang for one dollar. Perhaps this term came about from the deerskins that were traded out West. Another name for deerskin is buckskin.

The Chinese word *cash* would seem to be the likely origin of our word "cash," meaning bills and coins, but it really comes from the French (or Italian) words for a money box, *casse* (*cassa* in Italian).

WORD origin

Money ONLINE

Everything Kids'

Back   Forward

http://

Visit the Smithsonian Museum's Web site at
www.si.edu/organiza/museums/nmah/csr/cadnnc.htm
to get a look at coins from around the world.

FUN FACT

Up until 1933, you could take a U.S. dollar bill known as a "gold certificate," to a bank and exchange it for its value in gold. Until 1934, you could take "silver certificates" to a bank and exchange them for silver dollars. The U.S. government no longer promises that it has enough gold or silver to back up its money. The citizens of the United States have faith that the U.S. government can back up its money with gold, silver, land, and other assets.

For thousands of years gold was the accepted basis for determining value. It was the "standard" by which many developed their monetary systems. For a while, the United States was on a bi-metallic system (silver and gold), but, in the 1800s the United States officially went on the "gold standard." The United States backed up all the money it issued with its supplies of gold. The United States discontinued the gold standard in 1971. I guess you could say the U.S. monetary system is now based on the "good faith" standard!

Europe opened in 1189. The Europeans did not rush right out and start making paper money.

Improvements in presses used for minting coins made it more convenient for people to continue using metal money. There was little reason to investigate the use of paper money. When you have precious silver or gold in your pocket, why replace it with flimsy paper that can be torn or destroyed?

Pound for Pound

In England, money is based on pounds instead of dollars. The term "pound" came from the weight of one pound of gold.

By the 1600s though, so much gold and silver was circulating in Europe that people found it was easier to leave their money with someone else for safekeeping. Goldsmiths issued notes that told how much gold had been left with them. These notes were written on paper.

Money ONLINE

Everything Kids'

Back Forward

http://

Ron Wise's "World Paper Money Home Page" has several thousand examples of bank notes from all over the world. Go to:
http://aes.iupui.edu/rwise/

FUN FACT

Nails

Have you heard of a tenpenny nail? A tenpenny nail was one that was sold for ten pence. Nowadays, tenpenny refers to the size of a nail.

Banks were also places where money could be kept safely. With the development of banks came the paper bank note. The bank note was a promise that a customer could exchange the note for precious metals that were being stored at the bank. The first bank note was issued in 1661 by the Stockholm Banco in Sweden.

Each bank had its own type of note. Eventually, national or central banks took over the job of issuing notes so that there would be uniformity. National governments told their citizens that the notes were "legal tender." The convenience and reliability of paper money led to its acceptance.

Fun with Money

Plastic Bottle Piggy Bank

Here's a good way to reuse an old plastic bottle and save a few pennies too!

What you need:

> An empty plastic bleach bottle with a cap
> (bleach bottles work well). Rinse and soak
> the bottle to remove the label.
> Scraps of felt
> One pipe cleaner
> Two large buttons
> Four large corks, empty thread spools, or
> wooden candle cups
> Glue gun
> Scissors
> Craft knife
> Marker

Adult assistance needed: this activity requires using a craft knife

What you do:
1. Place the bottle handle side up. With the craft knife, cut a slot in the top as shown.
2. Cut two ears from the felt.
3. Wrap the pipe cleaner tightly around a pen or pencil to form a corkscrew tail. Carefully slip the tail off the pencil.
4. Using the glue gun, glue the cork legs, the button eyes, the ears, and the tail to the bottle.
5. Using the marker add snout holes to the bottle cap.

   Variation: for a spotted pig, cut circles from the felt and glue to the bottle.

Heads to Tails

What you need:
  Paper and pencil
  Ruler
  Sixty-four pennies

What you do:
1. Using the ruler, measure a square eight inches by eight inches on the paper. Make a mark at every inch.

2. Make a grid as shown.

3. Put an "X" through the four middle squares.

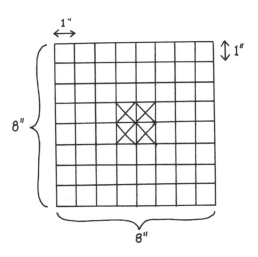

Fun with Money

How to play:

This is a game for two players. Each one will play with thirty-two pennies.

1. Decide who will go first. Player 1 will be "heads." Player 2 will be "tails." Player 1 will place two of his or her "heads" on two of the "X" squares. Player 2 will place two of his or her "tails" on the remaining "X" squares.

2. Player 1 then places a "heads" so that he or she has a "tails" between the two "heads." The move may be made horizontally, vertically, or diagonally. The "trapped" "tails" now is turned upside down to become a "heads."

3. Player 2 places a "tails" in a similar manner.

4. The play continues with each player placing his or her pennies so that the other's penny or pennies are "trapped" between. All "trapped" pennies must be turned over. All lines of pennies must be continuous. That is, there can be no skipped squares.

5. If a player cannot make a play, then the other player goes again.

6. The game ends when all sixty-four pennies have been played. Player 1 counts up all the "heads" pennies on the board. Player 2 counts up all the "tails." The player with the most wins.

Know someone who has trouble making change? Tell him or her about the "Cash Register Game" at www.funbrain.com/cashreg/index.html. It's a fun challenge that gets harder with each right answer you get!

Chapter 2
America's Coins

There was a shortage of coins in the American colonies during the seventeenth and eighteenth centuries. Colonists had to depend on non-coin types of money to conduct business. A number of colonies used wampum, tobacco, or other commodity money.

What was the reason for this shortage of currency? One reason is that money was sent back to England to buy things that weren't available in America. The goods were shipped to the colonies, and the money stayed in England. Another reason is that the British government did not want to send its coins to the colonies. It was a form of control.

Since ships came to the Americas from countries such as Portugal and France, coins other than English ones made their way into the economy. Due to trade with the Spanish West Indies, eight-reales silver coins became popular. These

Spanish milled dollars were also known as "pieces of eight" because they could be cut into eight parts, or "bits." Each bit was worth twelve and a half cents. Some of the Spanish dollars were minted in Mexico City from the rich supply of Mexican silver. The dollars were readily available to the colonists and were accepted for financial transactions. Another Spanish coin, the gold doubloon, was equal in value to sixteen of the silver dollar coins.

But still, there was not enough coinage to go around, and the colonies began to mint coins in smaller **denominations** to meet the demand for coins.

WORDS to KNOW

Denomination—a unit of value in currency—for example, 1 cent, 5 cents, $1, $20.

Obverse—the front of a coin ("heads").

Reverse—the back of a coin ("tails").

Counterfeiting—to make a copy of something. Counterfeiting is done with the intention of cheating someone. Counterfeiters make fake money and use it as if it were real—that is, until they get caught!

FUN FACT

The Salem witch trials took place in 1692 and at that time superstitious people wore bent coins as a way to protect themselves from witches. Many of the pine tree shillings that still exist show signs of having been bent!

Why did the workers at the Mint go on strike?

They wanted to make less money.

In 1652, John Hull of the Massachusetts Bay Colony, started a mint that produced very crude coins. The coins were stamped with NE for New England on one side and the denomination on the other. The simplicity of the coin led to trouble—it was easy to counterfeit and easy to clip. An improved design was necessary! From 1653 to 1674 Hull's mint produced redesigned coins that had a willow, oak, or pine tree on the **obverse** and the date and III, VI, or XII (the Roman numerals for 3 = threepence, 6 = sixpence, and 12 = shilling) on the **reverse**. Hull's coins are usually referred to as "New England pine tree" coins.

Other colonies began to mint coins too. There were different coins in each of the colonies. The values placed on the coins in each region also differed and often led to confusion. Benjamin Franklin, in his *Autobiography*, tells of going to a bakery in Philadelphia after his move from Boston:

> *Then I asked for a three-penny loaf, and was told they had none such. So not considering or knowing the difference of money, and the greater cheapness nor the names of his bread, I made him give me three-penny worth of any sort. He gave me, accordingly, three great puffy rolls. I was surpriz'd at the quantity, but took it, and, having no room in my pockets, walk'd off with a roll under each arm, and eating the other.*

Two Bits

You may have heard our quarter referred to as "two bits." This is a carryover from the old days of the Spanish pieces of eight. Two bits equaled twenty-five cents, a quarter of a dollar.

$ $ $

A Revolutionary War captain, Thomas Machin, set up a mint in New York in the late 1780s. He had contracts to mint coins for Vermont as well as Connecticut. Since so many different coins were in circulation at that time, Machin thought that a little **counterfeiting** wouldn't be noticed. He decided to mint some British halfpennies. Being a clever counterfeiter, he even produced his coins "pre-worn" so that people would think they had been around for years. Unfortunately, there was one place he wasn't so careful—in the minting process itself. It seems that several coins were made with a British halfpenny on one side, and a Vermont coin on the other!

WORDS to KNOW

Legend—the words on a coin.

Motto—a brief statement that usually expresses an ideal or goal.

Imagine how confusing things got by the end of the eighteenth century when the British had been defeated, and each of the states was minting its own coins! Take for example, Connecticut. During the years 1785 to 1788, more than three hundred different copper coins were made! Why so many? The state authorized private citizens to mint the coins for the state. Each developed its own design!

Individual states did not always find it easy to mint their own coins. In 1787 and 1788, when the state of Massachusetts began to make copper cents and half cents, it found that it cost two cents to make each cent, and one cent to make a half cent! Massachusetts only operated its mint for a short time!

A NATIONAL COIN

By 1787 it was time for the United States to think about producing a national coin. James Jarvis was given a contract by Congress to produce three hundred tons of copper coins.

Jarvis minted a coin known as the "Fugio" cent. The Fugio cent is the first official coin of the United States.

The cent had a sundial on the obverse and the Latin word fugio meaning "I fly," referring to the old saying, "time flies." Also on the obverse is the **legend**, "mind your business." Mind your business refers to the citizens of the United States having to build up their businesses to make for a stronger country. It had nothing to do with nosiness!

The reverse of the Fugio cent had a chain with thirteen links representing the thirteen states, and the **motto**, "we are one."

FUN FACT

Several stories are told about where the three hundred tons of copper used in the Fugio cents came from. One is that the copper was left over from the metal bands that held together powder kegs used in the Revolutionary War. Another is that many U.S. citizens including Benjamin Franklin donated their copper teapots!

The U.S. Constitution was adopted by Congress in 1791. One of Congress's first acts was to create the U.S. Mint. Construction of the building began shortly thereafter in Philadelphia. The Coinage Act of April, 1792 set up a system of coin denominations. Ten coins were chosen: a $10 gold eagle, a $5 gold half-eagle, a $2.50 gold quarter-eagle, a silver dollar, a silver half-dollar, a silver quarter-dollar, a silver-**disme**, a silver half-**disme**, a copper cent, and a copper half-cent piece. It also allowed for the coins to be minted with the legend, "United States of America."

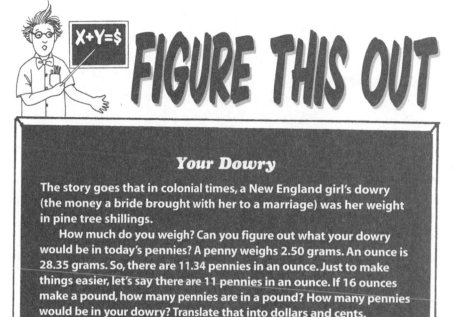

FIGURE THIS OUT

Your Dowry

The story goes that in colonial times, a New England girl's dowry (the money a bride brought with her to a marriage) was her weight in pine tree shillings.

How much do you weigh? Can you figure out what your dowry would be in today's pennies? A penny weighs 2.50 grams. An ounce is 28.35 grams. So, there are 11.34 pennies in an ounce. Just to make things easier, let's say there are 11 pennies in an ounce. If 16 ounces make a pound, how many pennies are in a pound? How many pennies would be in your dowry? Translate that into dollars and cents.

Before the construction of the mint building in Philadelphia was finished, 1,500 coins were produced by a private mint. It is believed that George Washington and his wife, Martha, donated some of their silver utensils for the minting. These first official coins were half-dismes dated 1792.

The following year, 1793, the Philadelphia mint started producing larger numbers of coins for general circulation. The first to be issued were the copper cent and half-cent pieces. It wasn't until 1796 that all the denominations were being made.

As the border of the United States expanded, the mint in Philadelphia was unable to keep up with the demand for coins. The first branch mints were set up in 1838. Today there are branches in San Francisco, California, Denver, Colorado, and West Point, New York.

Disme was another word for dime. It is uncertain if it was pronounced "dime" with the "s" silent, or "diz-me."

WORD origin

FUN FACT

Fun with Money

Take a handful of coins from your piggy bank and look for the mint marks. Why do you think mint marks are necessary? One answer is they are used for quality control. If there was a problem with coinage, the Treasury Department would need to know which mint to go to.

Plastic Pennies

Before it was decided to make the 1943 cent out of steel, other possibilities were investigated, including a penny made of plastic! The copper that was saved by not making copper pennies in 1943 was enough to make 250,000 shells for the military's big field guns!

Make a Wish?

People often make a wish and throw coins into pools of water. This practice can be dangerous to the animals that live in the pools or use them as a source of drinking water. Since 1982 the penny has been made of 97.6 percent zinc. The zinc that leaches out of the penny into the water is poisonous! So, please think twice before you make a wish and toss a coin!

The branches put mint marks on the coins they produced—an "S" for San Francisco, a "D" for Denver, and a "W" for West Point. Philadelphia has a mint mark "P", but it does not appear on cents or on coins made before 1980, with two exceptions—the 1942–45 nickels, and the 1979 Susan B. Anthony dollars.

Now that the United States had its own coins, all its money problems were over, right? Wrong! Unfortunately, not enough currency remained in circulation. It seems that the many silver and gold coins were sent to other countries by metals **speculators**. The coins were melted down and sold. The value of the metals in foreign countries was more than the value of the coins in the United States. This remained a problem until 1834 when Congress reduced the weight **standard** of its gold.

It wasn't until 1852 that Congress passed a law that allowed for coins to be minted with a metal value less than the face value of the coin. In other words, a silver dollar no longer had a dollar's worth of silver in it. The content of all the U.S. silver coins was reduced by 7 percent. A silver dollar after 1852 had a silver content of 93 percent, making it no longer profitable for metals speculators to ship the coins overseas.

Even though the United States had its own national coins during the period from the late 1790s until the 1850s, foreign coins continued to be used in the United States! In 1857 Congress finally outlawed the use of foreign currency as legal tender.

WORDS to KNOW

Speculator—a person who enters into a risky business arrangement in the hopes that a lot of money will be made in a short period of time.

Standard—a measure by which something can be compared and judged.

TYPES OF U.S. COINS

Today the following coin denominations are being circulated in the United States: one cent (penny), five-cent piece (nickel), ten-cent piece (dime), twenty-five cent piece (quarter), fifty-cent piece (half-dollar), and a dollar. There are no coins that are made of one metal—all U.S. coins contain alloys (mixtures of two or more metals).

COMMON CENTS

The half-cent copper piece was minted only until 1857. The coin we know as the penny is officially called a cent. "Penny" is a popular carryover from the days of the British copper pennies. The cents produced from 1793 to 1857 are known as large cents. The coin was even larger than our present day quarter!

Liberty is the symbol of America's freedom and independence. Her image was used on coins nearly a hundred years before her appearance as a statue in New York harbor.

The large cent was replaced by a cent piece the same size as the one we know today. Until 1909, the head of an Indian in a headdress was on the obverse. A wreath decorated the reverse. In 1909, for the 100th anniversary of Abraham Lincoln's birth, the coin was redesigned with the head of Lincoln on the obverse and two ears of wheat on the reverse. In honor of the 150th anniversary of Lincoln's birth in 1959, the wheat on the reverse of the cent was replaced by the Lincoln Memorial.

FUN FACT

The very first cent issued had an image of Liberty with wild flowing hair on the obverse. On the reverse was a chain with thirteen links surrounded by the words "United States of Ameri." The coin was soon redesigned to read "United States of America."

$ $ $

The Buffalo nickel brings up visions of herds of buffalo roaming the plains. The model for the design was an American bison named Black Diamond. Black Diamond didn't roam the plains. He lived at New York's Central Park Zoo!

$ $ $

The Native American portrait on the obverse of the nickel was based on three real people: Iron Tail, an Oglala Sioux; Two Moons, a Cheyenne; and Big Tree, a Kiowa. The coin's designer used features from all three men to make the one image that appeared on the coin.

THE NICKEL

The half-dime was only minted until 1873 and it was even smaller than today's dime. In 1866 the nickel five-cent piece was introduced. It was the first non-silver five-cent coin and was made of 25 percent nickel and 75 percent copper. Its common name, "nickel," came from its nickel content. The first nickel had a shield design on the obverse. In 1883 the shield design was replaced with a Liberty head.

The next big change in the nickel took place in 1913 with the introduction of the Indian head (obverse) or Buffalo (reverse) type nickels. The Jefferson nickel we know today was introduced in 1938 and has been relatively unchanged except for its metal content during the World War II period.

Fun with Money

Did you ever see a penny on the ground and pass it by because you thought it too small an amount to bother with? Next time pick that penny up! As of August 11, 1999, over 26,000 kids from 46 states and 5 countries had collected more than 3,890,000 pennies! The pennies were raised to help support conservation efforts in Southwest China, the Congo Basin, and the Bering Sea. Penny by penny those kids raised more than $38,900 between April and August 1999 in a program called Pennies for the Planet. To find out more go to *http://wwf.org/pennies/* or write to World Wildlife Fund, Pennies for the Planet, 1250 Twenty-fourth St., NW, Washington, D.C. 20037-1175.

In another penny-drive, school kids from all fifty states sent in their pennies to the Old Ironsides Penny Campaign and raised $150,000 toward new sails for the USS *Constitution*'s bicentennial in July of 1997.

The present day cent has only 2.5 percent copper in it—the other 97.5 percent is zinc. Up until 1982, the Lincoln cent was made up of 95 percent copper, except for the year 1943. That year the United States was in the middle of World War II, and supplies of copper were needed for the war. The 1943 penny was made of a low-grade carbon steel with a zinc coating to prevent rusting.

THE DIME

Since 1796 the dime has been continuously minted. For its first ninety-six years an obviously feminine Liberty appeared on the obverse. In 1892, with a series of coins known as "Barber" type (named for the designer of the coin), Liberty's appearance changed. She took on a more masculine appearance. Then, in 1916, Liberty appeared with a winged helmet on her head! It was thought that this image was of the Greek god Mercury and the dimes from 1916 to 1945 are known as Mercury type dimes. The Franklin Roosevelt dimes we use today were introduced in 1946, shortly after President Roosevelt's death.

THE QUARTER

Quarter-dollars, or quarters as we know them, have gone through many changes since 1796. There have been more than thirteen types, but except for the last type, the Washington head, all have had Liberty on the obverse and an eagle on the reverse. The Washington head was introduced in 1932 to honor George Washington's 200th birthday!

For 1976, in celebration of the U.S. bicentennial, a temporary reverse design appeared—a colonial drummer. The obverse also carried the double date, 1776–1976. The half-dollar and the Eisenhower dollar coins also went through a bicentennial redesign.

An exciting change to the quarter began taking place in 1999. In 1999 five new quarters were introduced as part of a program to celebrate all fifty states. The new coins will be introduced five per year for the next ten years. They are being released in the same order that the states signed the Constitution or entered the Union.

The design of these new coins was a cooperative effort. Drawings submitted by state governors were reviewed by the U.S. Mint and several other groups with the final design being approved by the secretary of the Treasury.

There were several restrictions placed on the

In the 1880s cheap paperback books sold for ten cents and were known as "dime novels." In England around the same time, cheap paperbacks were known as "penny dreadfuls."

Design Flaw

When the nickel was redesigned in 1883, the reverse also changed. The word "cents" was not included with the Roman numeral V, meaning 5. What the coin's designers didn't realize was that the nickel was nearly the same size as the $5 gold piece. Some dishonest people had the nickel goldplated and passed it off as a new $5 gold piece! Approximately 5.5 million nickels had been made before the mint recognized the problem and changed the design!

$ $ $

The first U.S. coin to have the inscription "In God We Trust" was an 1864 two-cent piece. It was produced for only nine years.

design. A bust (head and shoulders) of no person, living or dead, was to appear. No state flags or seals were to appear. It was suggested that landmarks, state symbols, historical buildings, and outlines of the state were all appropriate.

Delaware, having been the first to sign the Constitution, had the honor of being represented on the first release. The design chosen for Delaware's coin is of a colonial rider on a horse. The rider is Caesar Rodney. The image represents his ride to Independence Hall in Philadelphia in 1776.

The half-dollar, also known as the fifty-cent piece, has been made nearly every year since 1794. Quick, tell me whose image appears on the latest half-dollar issue? If you said John F. Kennedy you are correct. I don't know about you, but I see very few half-dollars. Most people find them too heavy!

DOLLAR COINS

Dollar coins were originally issued in silver, but in the late 1800s a gold dollar was also produced. The last 90 percent silver dollar appeared in 1935. In 1971 the Dwight D. Eisenhower silver dollar was introduced. This last of the silver dollars was only 40 percent silver! It was no longer produced after 1974.

A most interesting dollar coin, but right now not well respected, is the Susan B. Anthony coin. The Susan B. was first minted in 1979. A controversy raged when this coin was first released. People complained about its size. It was only slightly larger than the quarter, and it also had reeded edging. People thought the similarity to the quarter would be confusing and result in errors being made in making change, or that the coin would jam in vending machines. Some people objected to a woman being a replacement for George

Fun with Money

There's no time like the present to start a coin collection. If you chose to collect all fifty states' quarters, you could have a complete set by 2009, and it would cost you only $12.50!

Washington who appears on the paper dollar!

The public for the most part refused to use the new coin, and production ceased in 1981. Supplies of the coins were kept warehoused in vaults until 1993 when the U.S. Postal Service installed new vending machines in post offices. The machines for making change to purchase stamps gave the Susan B. Anthony coin as change for $5 bills. The Susan B. came back to life!

Today, there are more than fifteen transit systems around the country, including New York and Chicago, using the dollar coin in vending machines. The supplies in the government vaults dwindled until 1999 when there was some question as to whether the U.S. Mint needed to produce new Susan B. Anthony dollars to keep up with the demand!

Money ONLINE

Everything Kids'

http://

To learn more about the fifty states' coin program, go to the U.S. Mint site at *www.usmint.gov*

FUN FACT

Required by Law

There are several things that are required by law to be on all U.S. coins. On the obverse: "LIBERTY"; an impression emblematic of liberty; "In God We Trust"; and the date. On the reverse: the denomination; "United States of America"; "E Pluribus Unum" (Latin for "out of many, one"—meaning out of many states, one United States!); and coins larger than the dime must have a representation of an eagle. Of course, exceptions may be made as is the case with the fifty state quarters. On these the reverse sides will not have an eagle, and some of the inscriptions will flip sides! U.S. law also states that the design of no coin may be changed more often than once every twenty-five years.

FUN FACT

Mint Sandwich

Not all coins at the U.S. Mint start with the cutting of blanks from strip. One-cent pieces are struck on premade blanks purchased by the Mint. The Mint sends supplies of copper and zinc to the commercial manufacturers for blanking.

Take a look at a new quarter. Along the reeded edge you will notice a thin sandwich of metals. The dime, quarter, and half-dollar are all "cupro-nickel clad" coins. They start with a layer of copper sandwiched between two layers of a copper-nickel mixture. This sandwich is bonded together and rolled to the proper strip thickness for cutting into blanks.

$ $ $

Worn and mutilated coins that have been returned to the U.S. Mint are melted down, sent out to commercial manufacturers to be made into strip, and start life all over again!

The time for a re-evaluation of the one-dollar coin came about. The advantages to the use of a dollar coin were becoming more obvious. A coin will last twenty-five to thirty years. A paper dollar lasts only one and a half years! Even with the higher manufacturing costs of the coin—eight cents as compared with four cents for the paper—the greater life of the coin makes it an economically sound choice. The U.S. Government Accounting Office estimates that the government could save $395 million a year by making dollar coins.

President Clinton signed into law the U.S. Dollar Coin Act in December 1997. The law required the U.S. Treasury to place into circulation a new one-dollar coin similar in size to the Susan B. Anthony. The new coin must be golden in color and have a noticeably different edge.

The secretary of the Treasury was given the power to have the coin designed with the approval of Congress. The reverse must have an image of an eagle, but the image on the obverse was left up to the secretary.

A Dollar Coin Design Advisory Committee of seven was appointed by the secretary of the Treasury to suggest a subject for the obverse design. The secretary asked the committee to select a woman who was no longer living.

The public was invited to make suggestions, and they did— by mail, by phone, and through the U.S. Mint's Web site.

On June 9, 1998, the committee recommended that the new dollar coin have a design representing Sacagawea, the Native American (of the Shoshone tribe) woman who guided the Lewis and Clark expedition to the Pacific Ocean in 1804–1806.

The U.S. Mint invited twenty-three artists who had a knowledge of Native American culture and history to submit designs.

Jack: "Can you change a quarter for me?"

Jill: "Sure."

Jack: "Then change it into a dollar!"

Money ONLINE

Everything Kids'

To find out more about Sacagawea, visit the U.S. Mint Web site at *www.US mint.gov/dollarcoin/sacagawea.cfm*. Or look for *Sacagawea* by Judith St. George (Philomel Books, 1997) at your local library or bookstore.

> Why is the moon worth only a dollar?
>
> Because it has four quarters.

They submitted 121! The U.S. Mint narrowed the choices down to six obverse and seven reverse designs.

On December 7, 1998, the U.S. Mint published the designs on its Web site and invited comments. More than 120,000 e-mail messages and over 2,000 letters and faxes were sent in response! The Mint also consulted with focus groups and individuals to further narrow the choice of designs to three obverse and four reverse. The Secretary of the Treasury had to make the final decision.

His decision was announced live from the White House on May 4, 1999. First Lady Hillary Rodham Clinton made the announcement. She said, "How fitting that the first U.S. coin of the new millennium should carry the image of the Native American woman whose courage and quiet dignity provides such a powerful link to our past."

The new coin will be released in the spring of 2000. The obverse will have the image of Sacagawea looking over her shoulder and carrying her young son, Jean Baptiste. On the reverse will be a flying eagle surrounded by seventeen stars representing the number of states at the time of the Lewis and

FUN FACT

Fun with Money

Can you find the mushroom on the dollar bill? Hold a dollar bill face up. Press your fingernail in a line along the bottom of Washington's forehead. Fold the bill back along the line. Now, grasping the fold line bring it down over Washington's face. Stop at the chin and flatten the fold. Look at the bill. Do you see the mushroom?

FIGURE THIS OUT

At the mint, pennies are counted and put in canvas bags for shipping. Each bag holds $50 worth of pennies. How many bags did it take to bag up the 10,257,400,000 pennies produced by the U.S. Mint in 1997?

Clark expedition. The coin will have features that prevent its being confused with any other coin. It will also be acceptable for vending machine use.

HOW A COIN IS MADE

As you saw with the Sacagawea one-dollar coin, the design process is complex. What happens after the design has been approved by the secretary of the Treasury? A coin can be made! First, a **die** must be produced.

A sculptor-engraver at the U.S. Mint makes a model out of plasticene, a non-hardening type of modeling clay. The model is three to twelve times larger than the finished coin. Several plaster of Paris models are then made, and the final model is called a "galvano." With each step the models are adjusted so that all the necessary detail in the design sketches is reproduced. The final model must be approved by Mint officials before the process continues to the next step.

"Money is flat and meant to be piled up."
—*Swedish proverb*

The galvano is put on a machine called a transfer engraving machine. The machine cuts the design in a steel **blank** that is the same size as the finished coin, producing a hub. A hub is used to make the dies that **strike** the coins.

Actual production of the coins can now begin. First, large sheets of metal called coin strip, are fed into presses that cut out blanks, also known as planchets. The planchets are softened in a furnace in a process called annealing. They are then washed and dried, and put on a riddler to screen out coins of the wrong shape and size.

Next, the planchets are put through the upsetting machine. The upsetting machine forms the raised edges of the coins. During this stage the edges are hardened. The hardening is a necessary step. If the edges aren't hard when the coin is struck, some of the metal could squirt out!

After the planchets have been upset, they go to the coining presses. Set up in the coining press are the dies for both the obverse and the reverse. The planchet is struck only once to make a coin. Dimes, quarters, and half-dollars get reeded edges at the same time that they are struck.

The finished coins are inspected, counted, bagged, and then shipped off to Federal Reserve Banks for distribution.

WORDS to KNOW

Die—a tool for stamping out the design of a coin.

Blank—an unmarked piece of metal in the shape and size of a finished coin.

Strike—to impress a design on. This comes from the days when coins were actually struck using a hammer.

Chapter 3
A Brief History of
U.S. Paper Money

In Canada, in 1685, North America's first paper money was issued. Close your eyes and imagine the first French-Canadian notes. Do you picture a beautifully decorated paper note? Try again. Think deck of cards . . .

Supply ships were delayed in getting to New France, a part of Canada controlled by France. The governor of New France had no money to pay his soldiers so he used the only paper available to him—playing cards! The playing cards became "promissory notes" made official with seals and signatures. The notes were a promise to the soldiers that when the ships arrived the notes could be exchanged for real money.

The Canadian notes did not work as well as planned, but it didn't stop the colonists in Massachusetts Bay Colony from following Canada's lead. The Colony issued paper notes in 1690 to pay soldiers for their service against Canada in King William's War. The trouble with these "Old Charter" bills was that they were not legal tender. The only thing they could be used for was paying taxes!

Throughout the colonies coins were scarce and expensive to produce. A reasonable alternative was paper notes. Notes were printed in denominations as small as three pence! Most of the notes were issued in denominations based on the British monetary system, but some notes had values in Spanish dollars. Each colony produced its own notes, and like coinage in early America, paper money values varied.

Just prior to the Revolutionary War the colonists needed to raise money to pay for their fight against the British. The Continental Congress issued paper money called

FUN FACT

"Not worth a Continental" is a phrase that was once common in the United States. It meant something of little or no value.

$ $ $

You know that "Dixie" refers to the South, but did you know that the name Dixie comes from a ten-dollar bill? Before the Civil War, a bank in New Orleans issued $10 notes. Because both French and English were spoken in New Orleans, the denomination on the back of the bill was written in French, *dix*, meaning ten. The bills were used widely, and New Orleans became known as the land of Dix. Eventually the land of Dix, or Dixie, came to refer to all of the South!

How did
Barbie pay for
her new outfit?

With dolly bills.

"Continentals," with values in dollars, not British pounds! Unfortunately, the colonies had nothing to back up their money. The Continental Congress had planned on collecting taxes that would be used to back the notes, but the plan fell through. To add to the problem, the notes were easily counterfeited. All in all, the Continental was a failure.

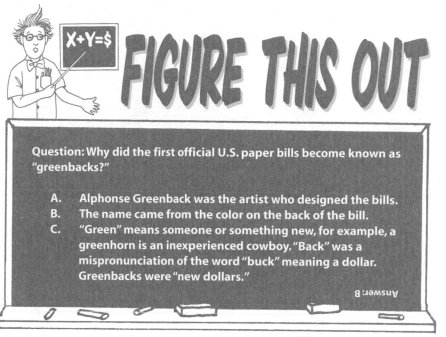

FIGURE THIS OUT

Question: Why did the first official U.S. paper bills become known as "greenbacks?"

A. Alphonse Greenback was the artist who designed the bills.
B. The name came from the color on the back of the bill.
C. "Green" means someone or something new, for example, a greenhorn is an inexperienced cowboy. "Back" was a mispronunciation of the word "buck" meaning a dollar. Greenbacks were "new dollars."

Answer: B

THE BANK OF THE UNITED STATES

It is difficult for us to imagine, but in the early years of the United States, the government was not in the business of issuing paper money. Paper money was issued by banks. The notes were promises that the bank would exchange the paper notes for their value in gold or silver coins.

The newly formed U.S. government attempted to put an end to some of the confusing money situations that had made life in the colonies difficult. In 1791, shortly after the adoption of the Constitution, the first Bank of the United States was **chartered** by Congress. Congress gave it the power to issue bank notes.

The banking business was rocky in the first half of the nineteenth century. The first Bank of the United States almost

WORDS to KNOW

Chartered—recognized by a government (federal or state) as being a business or organization. A charter is a document describing the purpose, the place of business, and other details.

Money ONLINE

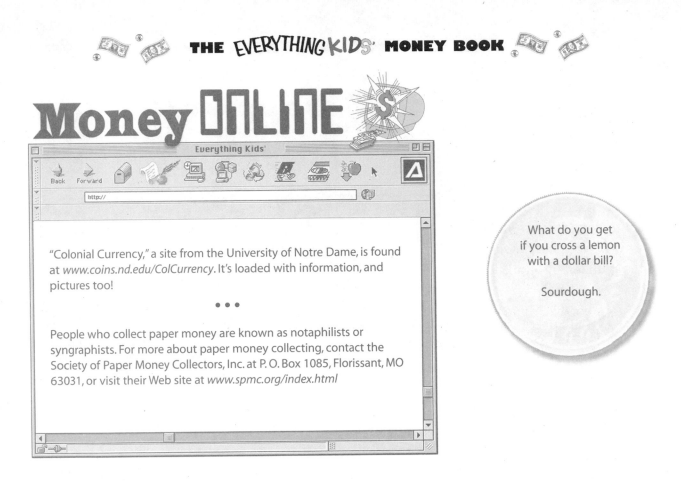

Everything Kids'

http://

"Colonial Currency," a site from the University of Notre Dame, is found at *www.coins.nd.edu/ColCurrency*. It's loaded with information, and pictures too!

• • •

People who collect paper money are known as notaphilists or syngraphists. For more about paper money collecting, contact the Society of Paper Money Collectors, Inc. at P. O. Box 1085, Florissant, MO 63031, or visit their Web site at *www.spmc.org/index.html*

What do you get if you cross a lemon with a dollar bill?

Sourdough.

didn't have its charter renewed by Congress in the 1810s! Congress rechartered the bank because it wasn't able to borrow enough money from state banks to pay for the War of 1812!

The charter came up for renewal again in the 1830s but this time Congress did not renew it. Once again, money-wise, the United States was in a big mess!

FUN FACT

The first United States Notes were printed by private printing companies. To make them legal, they had to be signed. In 1862, each note that was issued was signed, one by one. Two signatures were required on each note. Six Treasury Department employees did all the work!

BANK NOTES

States chartered many banks, but they did a poor job of regulating them. Almost anyone could start up a bank and print bank notes. Bank notes were printed without sufficient backing. By 1836 there were about 1,600 banks and over 30,000 different bank notes!

Banks failed frequently, especially in the Panic of 1837, when people went to the banks looking to exchange paper notes for gold and silver. Those banks that did not have the metal to back the notes went bankrupt. Today, paper money collectors call the bank notes from this time "broken bank notes" because most of the banks went broke!

By the start of the Civil War the banking system was in chaos. Coins were once again in short supply, and the United States had no reliable system by which it could pay for the war. Congress gave the U.S. Treasury the authority to issue "Demand Notes," or notes that would allow the holder of the note to demand payment.

The demand notes issued in 1861 were replaced the following year by United States Notes. The United States Notes, also known as "legal tender notes," were commonly referred to as "greenbacks."

"National Bank Notes" were formally allowed by Congress through the National Banking Act of 1863. They continued to be circulated until the 1920s. The stock market crash of 1929 brought about the end of the bank note in the United States.

In 1913, with the establishment of the Federal Reserve System, the "Fed" took over the issuance of paper money (see Chapter 5 for more on the Fed).

"Federal Reserve Notes" make up 99 percent of all paper money in circulation in the U.S. today.

The twelve Federal Reserve Districts and the letters and numbers that represent them on currency are:

Boston—1–A	Chicago—7–G
New York—2–B	St. Louis—8–H
Philadelphia—3–C	Minneapolis—9–I
Cleveland—4–D	Kansas City—10–J
Richmond—5–E	Dallas—11–K
Atlanta—6–F	San Francisco—12–L

FUN FACT

In times of war, a government fears that its currency might get into the hands of the enemy. This was the case in World War II. After the bombing of Pearl Harbor, the United States exchanged all of the paper notes in Hawaii for special notes that were printed with brown ink and had the word "Hawaii" on the front and back. If Japan had invaded the island, then the United States would have declared the special notes invalid. The notes would have been worthless on the world market. Since there was no invasion, the notes were considered legal tender and were used until 1944.

$ $ $

Salmon P. Chase appeared on the $10,000 bill. Never heard of Salmon P. Chase? Don't feel bad, most adults don't know who Salmon P. Chase was either. Go ahead, ask your mom or dad! So who was Salmon P. Chase?

Born in New Hampshire, Chase grew up to be a lawyer and later became secretary of the Treasury under Abraham Lincoln. He was responsible for the development of the greenback, our first official paper money! Chase also ordered "In God We Trust" to be added to U.S. coins. "In God We Trust" didn't appear on U.S. bills until 1957.

FIGURE THIS OUT

Americans don't seem to like the $2 bill and it is rarely seen, but in 1996 there were 102,400,000 printed. Whose picture appears on the $2 bill?

Answer: Thomas Jefferson

$ $ $

If there are 490 bills in a pound, what would be the dollar value of a ton of $5 bills?

Answer: $4,900,000

FUN FACT

How are paper notes printed? By a process called "engraving." The design is cut into a steel plate. Ink is put on the plate and it sinks into the grooves. The ink is then cleaned away from the surface of the plate. The plate is pressed against a sheet of moist paper and the ink from the grooves is transferred to the paper.

A paper note is printed three times: first the green back, second the face in black ink, and the third printing includes the Federal Reserve seal, the green Treasury seal, and the green serial numbers.

$ $ $

Counterfeiting has been a problem for as long as there has been money! In ancient Rome, counterfeiting was punishable by death. Counterfeiters had their hands cut off in eleventh-century England. An eighteenth-century New Englander lost his ears for the crime of counterfeiting!

Two other types of notes need to be mentioned—gold certificates and silver certificates. Gold certificates, starting in 1865, could be exchanged for gold coins or **bullion**. They were in circulation until 1933. Silver certificates could be exchanged for silver dollars starting in 1878. These bills remained in circulation until 1963, although they could not be exchanged for silver dollars after 1934.

Like the minting process, printing paper money takes place with high-speed machinery. Every day the Bureau of Printing and Engraving prints about 22.5 million Federal Reserve notes! It also prints U.S. postage stamps!

PAPER MONEY TODAY

In 1929, big changes were made in U.S. paper notes. The size was reduced by 25 percent to make the bills easier to handle, and the design was standardized for all the denominations. Very few changes were made until 1994, when paper currency was redesigned to add anti-counterfeiting and other features. These newly designed bills are being added over a period of years. The first to be introduced was the $100 note in 1996.

There are seven denominations of paper money currently being produced: $1, $2, $5, $10, $20, $50, and $100. At one time there were also $500, $1,000, $5,000, and $10,000 bills, but these haven't been printed since 1946. The largest U.S. bill is the $100,000, and only 42,000 were produced, all in 1934. The $100,000 bill was never in general circulation. It was used only for Federal Reserve Bank transactions.

What appears on the backs of the $2, $5, $10, $20, $50, and $100 bills?

Answer: $2—Monticello, Jefferson's home; $5—the Lincoln Memorial; $10—the U.S. Treasury building; $20—the White House; $50—the U.S. Capitol; $100—Independence Hall in Philadelphia.

Money ONLINE

Everything Kids'

Back Forward

http://

Did you realize that U.S. paper money has no wood fiber in it at all? The paper used in U.S. currency is made of 75 percent cotton and 25 percent linen. It also has tiny blue and red silk threads embedded in it. The paper is made by Crane and Company, Inc. and has been made by them since 1879! The formula is a secret, but one thing they will tell you is that it is made out of denim scraps—the same material that goes into your jeans! Paper made from scraps of fabric is known as "rag" paper. Besides making new paper for currency, Crane also recycles old shredded paper money into new writing paper! Visit their museum in Hingham, Massachusetts. Call 781-684-6481 for information about hours. Admission is free. If you can't visit in person, visit their Web site at *www.crane.com*.

WORDS to KNOW

Bullion—gold or silver in bar form.

READING A ONE-DOLLAR BILL

Let's take a look at both sides of a dollar bill to see what all the words, numbers, and pictures mean:

ON THE FACE

A. *"Federal Reserve Note"*—About 99 percent of all currency now in circulation are Federal Reserve Notes. These notes are printed to meet the demand of the Federal Reserve System.

B. *"The United States of America"*—Tells everyone that this paper money is from the United States. It also appears on the back of the bill.

C. *Federal Reserve District Seal*—Each of the twelve Federal Reserve Districts has its own seal. This bill comes from the Federal Reserve Bank in Boston. The large letter "A" is the letter specifying Boston.

D. *Serial number*—Each bill has its own serial number. No number is repeated within the

same denomination and series. Notice the letter at the beginning. It also refers to the Federal Reserve Bank. The letter at the end of the serial number refers to the print run. The first run is "A." In each run, the numbers go from 00000001-99999999. What run was this bill done on? A serial number with a star at the end tells us that the bill is a replacement for one that was destroyed during the printing process. These are referred to as "star notes."

E. This number appears four times on the front and refers to the Federal Reserve District.

F. *"This note is legal tender for all debts, public and private"*—The United States has decided that this currency is valid for the payment of all debts within the United States.

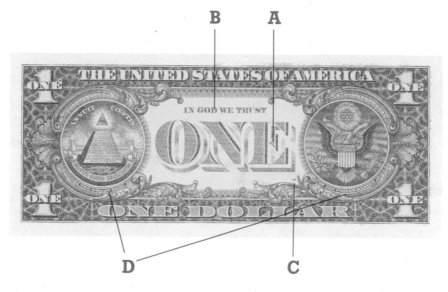

G. *Signatures*—There are always two signatures on the bill, one of the treasurer of the United States, and the other of the secretary of the Treasury.

H. *Treasury Department Seal*—The seal is printed in green ink over the denomination printing done in black.

I. *Check letter*—The letter is the same in both the upper left and lower right.

J. *Face-plate number*—The number of the plate used to print the bill.

K. *Quadrant number*—Where the bill appears on the sheet of thirty-two bills that come off the printing press.

L. *Denomination*—The denomination is spelled out twice, and appears as a number in the four corners.

M. *Portrait*—No living person may appear on U.S. currency. Presidents, in this case George Washington, appear on all the denominations currently being printed except for the $10 and $100 bills. Do you know who appears

on these? Answer: Alexander Hamilton on the $10, Benjamin Franklin on the $100. And in case you didn't know, the presidents on the other bills are, $2—Thomas Jefferson, $5—Abraham Lincoln, $20—Andrew Jackson, and $50—Ulysses S. Grant.

N. *Series*—Every time a new design is used or a new secretary of the Treasury is appointed by the president and approved by Congress, the series date changes. If a bill has a letter after the date, it means a very minor design change has been made, or a new treasurer has been appointed by the president.

ON THE BACK

A. *Denomination*—The amount is written out six times and written as a number four times.

B. *"In God We Trust"*—By law, this motto appears on all U.S. coins and currency.

C. *Plate number*—The plate used to print the back of the bill.

D. *The Great Seal of the United States*—The two sides of the Great Seal are reproduced on the one-dollar bill. On its obverse is the representation of the American bald eagle. E Pluribus Unum means "out of many, one." The number thirteen, representing the original thirteen states, appears several times—in the stripes on the shield, in the tail feathers, in the stars, in the arrows, and in the leaves and olives on the branch. The olive branch symbolizes peace. The arrows symbolize the fight for liberty, and the cloud and stars above the eagle's head represent God and the light shining in the darkness. On the reverse is a pyramid symbolizing strength, and like the pyramids of Egypt, long life. The pyramid is made of thirteen layers. It is unfinished to indicate that the United States continues to be built. The Roman numeral at the base is the number 1776. *Annuit Coeptis* is Latin for "He has smiled on our undertakings," meaning God has favored the United States. The eye represents the eye of God. The other Latin motto, *Novus Ordo Seclorum*, means "a new order of the ages." The new order refers to the new nation. The original Great Seal is made of brass (the one used today is made of steel) and is impressed into important papers to make them legal.

ANTI-COUNTERFEITING AND OTHER FEATURES

What is counterfeiting? It is making a copy of a note in an attempt to defraud (cheat).

During the Civil War period counterfeiting became so widespread it is estimated that by 1865 one-third of all U.S. paper money in circulation was counterfeit! The U.S. Secret Service was originally founded to combat this rash of counterfeiting.

In the late twentieth century, photocopiers, computers, printers, and scanners have made it easier for counterfeiters to make fake bills. The U.S. Treasury Department added some security features in Series 1990 notes, but more was needed, and a completely redesigned note was introduced with Series 1996. Let's take a look at the Series 1996 $20 bill:

The U.S. Secret Service was made a part of the U.S. Department of the Treasury in 1865. Within ten years, the activity of counterfeiters was way down. The Secret Service reports that during 1997, more than $136 million in counterfeit U.S. currency was discovered. Of that, 75 percent was seized before it got into circulation!

ON THE FACE

A. *Portrait*—The portrait displays the most changes. It has been moved slightly off center to prevent wear. Most bills are folded in half, and the portrait on old style bills becomes worn quickly. The portrait has been enlarged for easy identification, and background lines are printed in fine-line patterns that are difficult to reproduce.

B. *Watermark*—A watermark, a design impressed on the paper while it is being made, is in the space to the right of the portrait. If you hold the bill up to the light, you will see the same portrait of Jackson, but without the color!

C. *Federal Reserve Seal*—Rather than the seal of each of the twelve districts, one standard seal is used.

D. *Federal Reserve district letter and number*

E. *Serial number*—There is now an additional letter at the beginning of the number. The first letter is the series number. The second letter is the Federal Reserve District Letter.

F. *Denomination.* The denomination still appears as a number in the four corners, but all the numbers are different sizes. The "20" in the left bottom corner has "microprinting." The microprinting must be viewed with a magnifying glass to read the print. In case you don't have a magnifying glass, I'll tell you what it says: "U.S.A. 20." The print does not photocopy clearly, so it acts as an anti-counterfeiting device. The "20" in the bottom right hand corner is printed with a special color-shifting ink. Depending on the angle, sometimes it

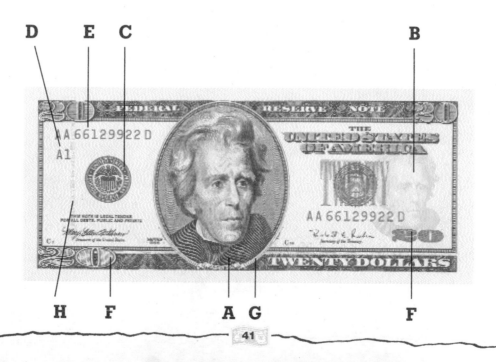

appears green, sometimes black. This feature is difficult to counterfeit.

G. *Microprinting*—Besides the microprinting in the numeral, microprinting also is found on the ribbon at the bottom of the portrait.

H. *Security thread*—If you hold the bill up to the light, you will see a line to the left of the Federal Reserve Seal. This line is a polymer strip (thread) that has been embedded in the paper. On the thread is more microprinting that has "U.S.A. TWENTY" and a flag. The security thread appears in a different place on each denomination. When under ultraviolet light, it glows a unique color for each denomination.

The first greenbacks were not made green for artistic reasons. Green was a color that did not reproduce well in early photography. Notes were green to prevent counterfeiting.

ON THE BACK

A. *Low-vision feature*—In the lower right hand corner, the larger "20" stands out against the light background and enables people with poorer vision to identify the denomination.

B. *Fine-line printing*—Like the background of the portrait, the background of the White House also is printed with fine lines to discourage counterfeiting.

The Treasury Department has also added some machine-readable features to the new bills so that vending machines, ATM machines, and so on will be better able to identify real bills and to reject fake ones. A machine-readable feature has been added to the $20 bill to allow for handheld currency readers to be made available to the visually impaired.

B   A

Read All About It!

For information about what appears on the other denominations, read Nancy Winslow Parker's *Money, Money, Money: The Meaning of the Art and Symbols on United States Paper Currency* (HarperCollins Children's Books, 1995).

FIGURE THIS OUT

Prior to the change in 1929, notes were 3.13 inches x 7.42 inches. Present day notes are 2.61 inches x 6.14 inches. About how many of these notes would it take to make a line a mile long?

Answer: 10,319

FUN FACT

Knock It Off!

Counterfeiting also occurs with coins, checks, credit cards, and consumer goods, such as watches! Counterfeit consumer goods are sometimes called "knockoffs."

Go Directly to Jail!

"Whoever, with intent to defraud, falsely makes, forges, counterfeits, or alters any obligation or other security of the United States, shall be fined under this title or imprisoned not more than fifteen years, or both." U.S. Code Title 18, Section 471.

$ $ $

The U.S. Treasury Department Web site *www.ustreas.gov* and the Bureau of Printing and Engraving site *www.bpe.ustreas.gov* will lead you to more information about U.S. paper money and how it is made.

Fun with Money

Physical Feats with Money

SNATCH A PENNY
Test your coordination with this stunt:

What you need:
    One or more pennies

What you do:
1. Put your hand palm up next to your ear (right hand next to right ear, or left hand to left ear). Your elbow should be in a horizontal position.
2. Place a penny on the top of your elbow. Quickly move your elbow in a downward motion. The penny will fall. Try to grab the falling penny out of the air.

    Practice the motions until you can do it easily. Are you ready for the next challenge? Two or more coins! Then try to place a line of coins from your elbow towards your hand. I hope you enjoy picking up pennies off the floor!

To begin any day right, you need a good breakfast. Why not plan a day of money fun and start it off with— SILVER DOLLAR PANCAKES! Measure pancake batter into a frying pan using a tablespoon. Your pancakes will be the size of a silver dollar I bet you'll have no trouble eating $10 worth! For variety, add a slice of banana to each pancake while cooking the first side.

According to the Guinness Book of World Records, in 1993 an Englishman named Dean Gould snatched 328 British ten-pence pieces in one flip of the arm!

Chapter 4
Banks and the Business of Money

BANKING HISTORY

Banks have been around almost as long as there has been money. Evidence of **loan** activity from about four thousand years ago has been found on clay tablets in Babylonia and Assyria. The Code of Hammurabi, a king of Babylonia during the eighteenth century B.C. included laws having to do with banking.

In ancient times temples were considered safe places for keeping money. Temples collected and stored large amounts of precious metals, as well as grains and other commodities. No one would dare anger the gods by trying to break into the temple treasury!

The Egyptians developed a system of banking using grains. In this system, a central grain bank in Alexandria recorded all the deposits made in Alexandria and in other state granaries. Grain owners began writing up orders so that their grain could be used to pay off debts. For example, if someone needed to pay his taxes, he wrote up an order for a certain amount of grain to be taken and given to the tax collector. **Credit transfers** also took place in much the same way as money is transferred in banks today.

Italy appears to be the birthplace of banking as we know it today. In the ninth century a bank was begun in Lombardy, a section of northern Italy. Then, in 1407, the Bank of St. George opened in Genoa, Italy. It was in business for nearly four hundred years.

The Banco di Rialto, the first public bank, was started in Venice by an act of the Senate in the 1580s. This bank acted as

WORDS to KNOW

Loan—a sum of money given to a person with the understanding that it will be paid back with **interest**.

Interest—an amount charged for the use of money.

Credit—an amount in an account equal to the value of the commodity put in.

Transfer—to move from one account to another

Deposit—money put into a bank.

Eye to Eye

You're probably familiar with another law of Hammurabi's Code—"An eye for an eye, and a tooth for a tooth."

The word "bank" comes from the Italian word *banca*, which means bench. The earliest banking transactions were done at benches or tables.

WORD origin

a depository bank. That is, it kept safe the funds **deposited** by its customers. Its customers could demand the money back at any time.

The next development in banks was the exchange bank. An exchange bank worked differently than a depository bank. Gold or coins were put into the bank by a customer. The customer was given credit for the value of the deposit. The customer could then instruct the bank to pay another person or business in an amount up to the amount the customer had on credit. One of the first exchange banks, opened in 1609, was the Bank of Amsterdam in the Netherlands.

Finally, banks started issuing bank notes. As we saw in the last chapter, banks and the development of paper money went hand in hand!

> How does someone in Prague pay bills?
>
> With a Czech.

BANKING TODAY

Today there are many banks and banking services available. They include:

- *Savings and loan, commercial, and full-service banks*—offer a range of services including savings, checking, loans, safe deposit boxes, and **investing.**
- *Credit unions*—are formed by groups of people (members) having something in common—for example, the people who work in a large company. The credit union operates like a bank, but it is able to offer lower lending rates to its members.
- *Investment banks*—**underwrite** businesses by purchasing **stocks** and **bonds**.

WORDS to KNOW

Investing—spending money to make more money. You can spend your money on stocks, bonds, collectibles, or other investment options.

Underwrite—to be financially responsible for. For example, when new stocks (or bonds) are offered to the public, an underwriter agrees to purchase them. The investment bank then sells the stock to the public through a stock exchange.

Stocks—a share in a business.

Bonds—a way for governments or businesses to pay for long term projects. The bond is sold to an investor at less than its face value. After a fixed amount of time, the investor may redeem, sell back, the bond and receive the face value. For example, the U.S. government issues savings bonds. A Series EE $100 bond is purchased for $50. If the buyer holds on to it for seventeen years, it can be redeemed for its face value of $100.

Money ONLINE

Everything Kids'

http://

If you'd like to see a picture of a bond issued during World War II, go to *www.mafh.org* and click on "wallpaper." The bond from 1942 is decorated with Disney characters! War bonds were sold to the public to raise money to fight the war.

FUN FACT

Disappearing Coins

When you were younger did you think that if you took one hundred pennies and ten dimes and put them into a bank, you'd get those same pennies and dimes back? When I was a kid, there were still some silver dollars around. Several of my friends were very disappointed when they put their silver dollars in the bank and later got back paper money. I'll bet they're even more disappointed now with silver coins being so valuable!

$ $ $

Bankrupt comes from the word for bench, *banca*, and the Latin word for broken, *rupta*. Bankrupt means broken bench. If a banker failed, his bench was broken! Do you think the broken bench is related to "broke," meaning without money?

SAVINGS ACCOUNTS

You may already have a savings account. There are two types of simple savings accounts. One is known as a "passbook" account. When you sign up for this kind of account, you get a little book, a passbook, that you bring to the bank with you. In it, your transactions, what you put in and take out, and the interest your money earns are recorded.

The second type is a "statement" account. Your transactions and interest appear on a printed record, a statement, which is mailed to you each month or quarter (every three months).

Some other savings plans you should be aware of are Money Market Accounts, Individual Retirement Accounts, known as IRAs, trust accounts, and certificates of deposit.

Money Market Accounts pay a higher rate of interest, allow you to write a limited number of checks each month, similar to a checking account, but they require you to keep a certain amount of money in the account at all times.

An IRA helps a person prepare for the future. Perhaps it's a little early to be preparing for your retirement, but it's not too early for your mom and dad! The interest earned in an IRA is not taxed by the government until after you retire. This is considered good because then your taxes should be lower than when you were still working.

A new kind of IRA, called an Education IRA, is not for retirement at all. It is for future education costs. Ask your parents to investigate an Education IRA account that allows you or your parents to put away up to $500 a year toward college. The interest on this account is not taxable if it is used to pay for college costs.

Trust accounts are sometimes set up by parents for their children. The parents plan for the worst, their deaths. If they die before their children are old enough to take care of their own finances, then arrangements have already been made for the bank to manage the minor's (someone under legal age) money.

Certificates of deposit are also known as CDs. They are not plastic disks that you stick in a boombox or a D drive! A CD is a piece of paper, a certificate, that is a bank's promise to repay the holder. CDs pay a higher interest rate than a regular savings account. These are some rules that the holder must follow in order to get the interest:

Why is a river rich?

It has two banks.

1. A specified amount such as $1,000 must be deposited.
2. The money must not be taken out for a fixed amount of time—for example, six months, eighteen months, or three years. The longer the fixed amount of time, usually the better interest it pays.

FUN FACT

In 390 B.C. the Gauls, people from the area we know today as France and Belgium, attacked Rome. A flock of geese set up a noisy honking and alerted the Romans. In gratitude, the Romans built a shrine to the goddess of warning, Juno Moneta. The shrine was next to a building where coins were made. The Romans made a connection between the shrine and the mint, and as a result, both the words money and mint came from the name Moneta.

$ $ $

In the New Testament we hear of Jesus going to the Temple and overturning the tables of the moneychangers. What were moneychangers doing in the Temple?

If a worshipper wished to make a sacrifice, he needed to buy a sacrificial animal. If he had come from a place other than Jerusalem, he might not be carrying shekels, a type of silver money used in Jesus' time. The moneychangers were in the business of exchanging foreign money for shekels.

3. If the money is removed before the time is up, then the holder forfeits (gives up) some of the interest! This is called a penalty.

The bank pays more interest on a CD than a savings account because it knows it will have your money to use for a set period of time. With a savings account there is no guarantee that you won't close (take out all the money) the account tomorrow!

If you don't have a savings account, perhaps you should think about getting one. Why?

- Because a savings account pays interest on your money. Your money grows! Mold is the only thing your money will grow if you keep it under the mattress!
- Your money is safe. Can you guarantee that no one will ever get into the money you have stashed in a piggy bank? You might ask, "What about bank robbers?" Banks have insurance to cover bank robberies. "What if the bank fails and goes out of business?" If your account is kept in a Federal Deposit Insurance Corporation (FDIC) bank it is insured up to $100,000. The FDIC is run by the U.S. government and guarantees that you will not lose your savings. The important thing is to make sure that the bank that you use is a member of the FDIC. FDIC banks usually have "Member-FDIC" notices posted where they can be easily seen. If you want to find out more, go to the "Learning Bank" at *www.fdic.gov/about/learn/learning/index.html.*

Account Details

So you've decided to open an account at your local bank, what do you do next? If you're under eighteen, you must have a parent or a guardian open the account with you. You will also need your social security number. What? You don't know it! Ask your parents if they claim you as a dependent on their income tax form. If they do, then they must have a social security number for you. They probably got one for you years ago, but you just didn't know about it!

At the bank you will be asked to fill out some forms, including a signature card. A signature card has a place for you to sign your name. When you take money out of your account, the teller may check the signature on your withdrawal slip against the one on your signature card. If they match, then the bank can be pretty sure they are giving the money to the owner of the account.

Social Security—a government program that pays money to people over the age of sixty-three, and to people with handicaps who can't work. The money for the program comes from employers and employee wages.

- You will develop a saving habit. Did you know that the United States is one of the worst countries when it comes to saving money? In 1998 only .5 percent of the money Americans had available after taxes went into savings. That means for every $1 that Americans earned, we saved only one-half of one cent!

INTEREST

Interest, in the case of a savings account, is the money a bank pays you for using your money!

The bank is in business to make money, so how does it make money if it is paying you? It makes money through its other services, one of which is lending money.

A bank lends money to individuals and businesses that qualify for a loan. That is, the bank checks to make sure the borrower can pay the money back! The bank does not just hand over the money to the borrower either. A contract must be signed. Part of the contract covers interest. Interest is the money a borrower pays to the bank for the use of the bank's money. The bank's money is the money you put into the bank!

The interest charged to the borrower is greater than the interest the bank gives you on your savings account. The bank uses the money it gets from loan interest and from fees to cover its expenses such as building mainte-nance, workers salaries,

The word "mortgage" comes from the French words *mort* meaning "death" and *gage* meaning "pledge." If the borrower of a loan pays it back, then the debt is "dead." If the borrower does not make the payment, then the lender gets to take the borrower's property. The property is "dead" to the borrower!

WORD origin

WORDS to KNOW

Withdrawal—money taken out of an account.

advertising, and so on. The bank's owner hopes that enough is left over to make a profit!

CHECKING ACCOUNTS

Most kids do not get checking accounts until they go off to college or get a job. When the time comes to open that first account you want to be prepared for all that is involved—finding the right account, understanding how to fill out a check, and so on.

A check acts as a substitute for cash. It means that in the check writer's bank account there is an amount of money equal to, or greater than, the amount written on the check. The check allows the money from the check writer's bank to be transferred to the payee.

Checking accounts are "demand deposit" accounts. That is, you as the account owner can demand your money in the form of a check by transferring the funds, or by making a **withdrawal**.

Let's examine the front of a check.

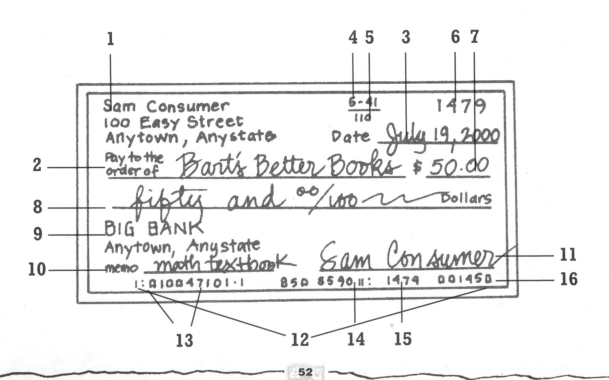

1. *Name and address*—This information identifies the owner of the account, the "drawer." The amount on the check is withdrawn from the account on the authority of the drawer.
2. *Pay to the order of*—This is where you put the name of the person or business that is to receive the check. The person is the "payee." When filling out this section, it is best to print. Cursive tends to be harder to read. It is also recommended that you spell out the name completely to make it harder to change.
3. *Date*—Show the date the check was written.
4. *Transit number*—This hyphenated number identifies the bank. The first number is either the city (numbers 1–49) or the state (numbers 50–99) the bank is in—for example, 1 = New York City or 54 = New Hampshire. The second number identifies the particular bank in the city or state.
5. *Check routing symbol*—Only those banks that belong to the Federal Reserve's check clearing system will have one of these district numbers.
6. *Check number*—The number of the check as it appears in the drawer's checkbook. This number may also appear in magnetic ink at the bottom.
7. *Amount of the check*—This is written as a number.
8. *Amount of the check*—The amount is written out in words for the dollar amount and a fraction for the cents. Fill up the whole line so that the amount can't be altered, or draw a line through any remaining space. In the case that the numerical and written amounts disagree, the bank goes by the written amount.
9. *Name of the bank*—This is your bank, where you put the money that this check is being written against.
10. *Memo*—This space can be used to remind you what you wrote the check for—for example, "birthday gift."
11. *Signature*—The name should be the same as the signature on the card that was signed when the account was opened. It must be written in ink so that it can't be altered.
12. *Magnetic ink character recognition*—The numbers along the bottom of the check are in special magnetic ink so that they can be read by machines that sort and process the checks.

FUN FACT

Don't Bounce!

You should never write a check for an amount more than you have in your account! If you do, it could be a very costly experience. For example, if you sent a check to Bart's Better Books and there wasn't $25 in your account, Bart will be charged a fee by his bank because it was not able to get the money from your bank.

Meanwhile, your bank will also charge you a fee because there was not enough money in your account; this is referred to as "insufficient funds." Your bank had to send the check back to Bart's bank—the check "bounced."

You still have to pay Bart for the book, but you will also owe him an extra amount to cover the fee he had to pay. So you end up paying two service fees! Chances are you will end up paying more in fees than the price of the book! And, if Bart ever sees another order from you, he may refuse to fill it. He no longer has faith in you!

Just one thing more, most times checks bounce unintentionally—maybe you made a mathematical error in your checkbook that made you think you had more money than you do—but knowingly writing a "bad" check is ILLEGAL!

FIGURE THIS OUT

The Rule of 72

You can double your money simply by keeping it in a savings account. How long will it take? The rule of 72 will help you figure it out. Say you have $100 in your savings account earning 3 percent interest. Take 72 and divide it by the interest rate, 3. You will get 24. In 24 years, your $100 will have grown into $200! Of course, the higher the interest rate, the faster your money will double. Check with your bank to find out the interest being paid on your savings, then use the rule of 72 to find out how fast your money will double!

FUN FACT

Fees Galore

Bank fees include charges for using ATM machines, check processing, late payments, annual fees for credit cards, and so on.

Vary Interesting

Here's an example of the varying interest rates for banking services at one bank. The interest paid to the owner of a statement or passbook savings account is 2 percent. The interest charged on a new car loan (with the loan to be paid back within 1 to 3 years) is 9 percent. The interest on a mortgage loan (with the loan to be paid back in 30 years) is 7.5 percent.

Mortgage

A mortgage loan has to do with the purchase of property such as a house. When you think of a mortgage remember compound interest. You get charged interest on both the principal and the interest. Over thirty years the interest paid to the bank really adds up!

13. *Routing number*—This is similar to the hyphenated number at the top of the check and identifies the bank for electronic transactions.
14. *Checking account number*—This identifies the account that the money will be taken (drawn) from.
15. *Check number*—This is the same as the number on the top of the check.
16. *Encoded amount*—The first bank that handles the check (either **cashes** it or credits it to an account) prints the amount in magnetic ink.

When it comes time to open your first checking account, you will find there is more than one type of account to pick from.

What's in a name? James Cash Penney was the perfect name for someone who started one of America's largest chains of department stores— J. C. Penney.

WORDS to KNOW

To cash—to receive paper money or coins in exchange for a check.

The first kind is the personal checking account. These accounts do not pay interest on the money kept in the bank, and fees are usually charged for check processing.

A second type of checking account does pay interest. In most cases you will have to maintain a minimum balance. That is, the bank specifies an amount, it could be $500 or more, that must remain in the account at all times. If you write a check that lowers your balance below the minimum, then you will not receive interest, and you will have to pay a monthly service charge.

There are many different checking accounts to choose from, so it is wise to have someone at your bank explain them to you.

How do checks work? Let's say your mom's birthday is coming up. You see an interesting book in a Bart's Better Books catalog that you know your mom will like. You fill out the order form. You must include payment, but it is unsafe to send cash through the mail, so you write a check. You send the $25 check to Bart's Better Books. Bart believes that you sent the check in "good faith." That is, you have enough money in your account to cover the amount of the check. Bart deposits the check in

Checks Galore

Don't have a checking account? You can still pay with a check in one of the following ways:

1. At a bank, you can ask the teller for a "cashier's check" in the amount you need. The teller will charge you for the amount of the check plus a small service charge. A cashier's check is also known as a bank money order.
2. Postal money orders are similar to bank money orders, but are purchased at post offices.
3. Traveler's checks are not really checks, but are a substitute for money. You can buy them in set denominations such as $20 or $100 and use them as you would cash. The advantages to traveler's checks are that they are widely accepted around the world, and if they are lost or stolen, they can be replaced.

his business bank account and sends you the book.

If the check you wrote is drawn on the same bank as the one that it is deposited into, then the transfer of funds is rather easy. This kind of check is called an "on-us" check because all the processing is done by "us"—that is, all by the same bank. About one-third of all checks are "on-us." The remaining two-thirds of checks are called "transit" checks because they move between banks.

Transit checks have a more complicated process. Checks may be sent to the Federal Reserve System check collection network or to a local clearing house.

Bart's Better books, a customer of Bank "A", brings in your check to Bank "A" to deposit. The check is to be drawn on your bank. We'll call your bank "Z". Bart's account is credited with the amount of your check (+ $25). Your check is then encoded with the amount to be drawn on your bank account (– $25). The checks then go to the central processing area for Bank "A" where they are sorted. On that day, Bank "A" has received checks that have to go back to Banks B, C, D, X, Y, and Z. In the sorting process, the checks are separated into piles of checks for B, checks for C, checks for D, and so on.

A courier (messenger) takes the sorted checks to a central meeting place, perhaps the local clearinghouse, where couriers from many banks exchange checks. The courier from Bank "A" gives checks to the couriers from B, C, D, X, Y, and Z, and receives Bank "A" checks from each of them in exchange.

Not all that long ago, checks had to be sorted by hand. Nowadays, check sorting is done by high-speed machinery. At the Boston Federal Reserve Bank, two to three million checks are processed each day!

FUN FACT

How does the right amount of money come out of an ATM? The machine has a cash dispensing mechanism that contains an electric eye. The electric eye counts each bill. The machine also has a sensor that checks the thickness of the bill to make sure two aren't stuck together. The sensor also picks out damaged or folded bills. Any bill that the sensor detects as abnormal is sent to a reject bin!

An Eye on ATMs

In order to make ATM use safer, research is being done in "biometrics." Biometrics are security measures using fingerprint, face, or voice recognition. One method of identifying a person is by the eye. The iris of your eye never changes, but your fingerprints or your face may change. Iris recognition devices may soon replace typing your PIN number at the ATM machine!

It may seem a little odd, but some people collect old checks! The American Society of Check Collectors has a Web site at *http://members.aol.com/asccinfo.* "Check" it out!

When your check reaches Bank "Z" the amount of your check is deducted from your account. When the next statement is mailed to you, you will receive your **canceled check**.

If you receive a check and you wish to cash it or deposit it in your account, you must first "endorse" it. To endorse is to sign your name on the back of the check. By signing it, you are letting the bank know that you are the person authorized by the check to be paid.

Checks can be endorsed in several ways:

1. *Blank endorsement*—A simple signature.
2. *Restrictive endorsement*—The endorser places a restriction on the transfer of money. In this case, the endorser wants the money to go into an account, rather than receive cash. You might write "For Deposit Only" under your signature, along with an account number.
3. *Special endorsement*—The endorser is giving another person the right to receive the money. Why would you do this? Say you owe $10 to your friend, John Smith. The family you mow lawns for pays you with a check for $10. Rather than cash the check, you can simply endorse it "pay to the order of John Smith."

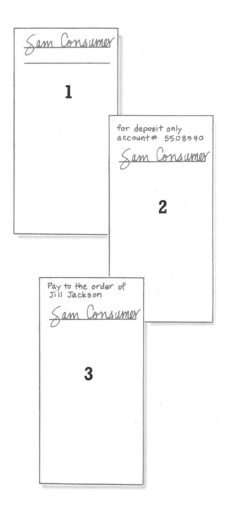

AUTOMATIC TELLER MACHINES

You know them as ATMs. When you were younger you probably thought they were magic money machines. Your mom or dad put in a little plastic card, punched in some numbers, and out popped the cash!

They're a bit more complex than that! The ATM machine is connected to the bank's central processor (computer) by telephone lines. When you put your card in the machine, it reads the magnetic strip on the back and makes sure that the information relates to the bank. If it is a valid card, you are asked to put in your "Personal Identification Number," known as your PIN. Your PIN is a "secret" number known only to you. This lets the machine know that you are the owner of the account being accessed.

At that point you may do a number of different banking functions. You can look at your balance (the amount remaining in your account), make a deposit, or withdraw money. Some machines are even equipped with U.S. postage stamps—you can do your banking and buy stamps without using cash!

If you withdraw money, the machine checks to see that there is enough in the account. ATM machines have a daily withdrawal limit, and some also deduct a fee for using the ATM. All transactions are recorded on a receipt that comes out of the machine when you have finished. Keep the receipt so that you can update your checkbook.

How do you stop an elephant from charging?

You take away his credit card.

FUN FACT

Safety Tips for Using an ATM

1. Never use an ATM that is not in a well-lit public place.
2. Never give your PIN number to anyone! If there are people around while you are typing in the number, stand in front of the keyboard so their view of what you are doing is blocked.
3. Never stand around the ATM and count your money—wait until you are back in your car, or at home. If you feel you have received the wrong amount, you may notify your bank. The bank will look at the journal that records each transaction done on the machine and try to clear up the mistake.
4. Remember not to leave your transaction record behind!

WORDS to KNOW

Debit—an amount that is subtracted from an account. It represents a debt, or an amount owed. The opposite of a debit is a *credit*. A credit is an amount added to an account.

A bank may join a network that enables its customers to use ATMs at locations far from the home bank.

DEBIT CARDS

Some ATM cards may also be used as debit cards. You can use a debit card instead of cash at stores and gas stations. When you swipe your card in the card reader, and put in your PIN, your checking account is immediately adjusted to reflect the amount of the **debit**. In other words, the money is removed from your bank account.

"Money may not buy love, but it sure can add zest to the shopping."
—*Henny Youngman*

ELECTRONIC BANKING

Electronic funds transfer, EFT, involves a nationwide communications/computer network where a large number of banks and businesses transfer money between accounts. For example, an employee (worker) is paid weekly by check. The check must be brought to the bank to be deposited. Between

FUN FACT

It's Confusing!

Electronic funds transfers are also known as automatic funds transfers. Transfers through the Automated Clearing House Network, a nationwide system of more than thirteen thousand banks, are referred to as ACH transfers.

EFT is also used by people who want to pay bills without writing checks. An arrangement is made between the person owing money, the business doing the billing, and both of their banks, so that funds are automatically transferred from one account to another.

Money ONLINE

Everything Kids'

http://

If you have a home computer you may want to consider "electronic banking." Electronic banking allows you to pay bills, check on your account balance, and transfer money between accounts. Check with your bank to see if this service is available.

WORDS to KNOW

Goods—products you can buy such as groceries, books, or camping equipment.

Services—work done for others. The person performing the service is paid for his knowledge and/or skill. For example, a doctor performs the service of healing, an auto mechanic fixes cars, and a clown entertains.

Asset—anything owned that can be converted into cash to cover your debt. For example, if you owned a hundred shares of stock in Microsoft, they would be considered an asset. The stock could be sold and converted into cash. Cash itself is an asset!

the time the employee receives the check and he or she gets to the bank, the check could be lost or stolen. But, with EFT, the employee is able to have the amount of the paycheck credited to his or her checking or savings account. This is referred to as "direct deposit." The amount credited is immediately available so that the employee can write checks or withdraw money. The employee gives the employer written permission to do this. Rather than having to write out a check and have it signed each week, the employer simply arranges to have the money transferred from the business account to the employee's account. Both employer and employee benefit.

PLASTIC

I'm sure you've heard credit cards referred to as "plastic." The reason for this is obvious. The cards used to charge **goods** and **services** are made of plastic. But before we talk about plastic, let's talk about credit. Credit is an arrangement between the seller and the buyer. The seller agrees to trust the buyer to purchase something, leave with it, and pay for it later. The seller is rewarded for his trust by prompt payment, or, if payment is not on time, the seller charges an additional amount called interest.

There are different kinds of credit arrangements. One is the installment plan method of buying. Say your parents want to buy an expensive item such as a new dishwasher. The store allows them to make a down payment; that is, a certain percentage of the total price is paid up front. Then, over a period of months or years, your parents pay off the rest of the purchase

"Credit" comes from the Latin *credo* meaning "to believe." The seller believes that the buyer will eventually pay!

WORD origin

cost, plus interest. If they fail to make the payments, the seller gets to take the item back, "repossess" it, and sell it to someone else.

Charge accounts are credit issued by individual stores or chains. These accounts come with credit cards that are only good at that particular store or one of its branches.

Major credit cards (Mastercard, Visa, Discover, and American Express are the most popular) allow you to buy goods and services at any business that accepts the particular credit card you have.

Credit and credit cards are not given to everyone. Businesses carefully screen out people who are a credit risk. How do they do this? They have a person fill out forms listing **assets**, employer, yearly income, credit information such as other credit cards owned, loans currently being paid off, and so on.

Who would have thought that the business of money is so complicated? Don't feel bad if it's all a little confusing. It's confusing to adults too! By reading this far, I'd say you're well on your way to becoming an informed banking customer.

In 1997 more than 283 million electronic bill payments were made in the United States! In 9 months, October 1998 through June 1999, the U.S. Treasury made almost 678 million payments (salaries, benefits, bills, and so on) electronically! That's 67 percent of the total payments made. The other 33 percent were made by check.

Fun with Money

Penny Relay

Want to have fun at a party? Divide the guests up into even teams and have a penny relay race!

What you need:

Two bowls for each team

Ten pennies per team

A disposable plastic spoon for each contestant

Two tables, one placed at each end of the room

What you do:

1. Put each team's pennies in its team bowl on the first table. This is the start bowl.

2. Place an empty bowl for each team on the second table. This is the finish bowl.

3. One person from each team should stand about two feet away from the start table. A second person should stand about two feet away from the finish table. The rest of each team equally spaces itself between the first and second team members.

4. Each contestant holds a plastic spoon with his or her teeth. No hands may be used during the relay except where noted in step six.

5. At the word "Go!" team member 1 dips the spoon into the bowl of pennies and scoops up one penny. If more than one penny is scooped up, the extra must be returned to the start bowl without using hands. Team member 1 then passes the penny to teammate 2. Team member 2 passes it to 3, 3 to 4, and so on. The last person in line puts the penny in the finish bowl.

Fun with Money

6. As soon as teammate 1 has passed the penny to 2, he or she goes back to the start bowl to get another penny and starts passing this one. If a penny is dropped anywhere along the line, it is picked up (this is the only time that hands may be used) and put back in the bowl at the start position.

7. The relay continues until one team gets all its pennies in the bowl at the finish line.

Variation: If there are not enough people to make teams, have individual contestants scoop up a penny at the start, run to the finish bowl, leave the penny, then run back to the start bowl to get another. The first person to get all ten pennies in his or her finish bowl is the winner. Dropped pennies must be picked up and returned to the start bowl.

Read All About It!

Demi has written and illustrated a delightful book called *One Grain of Rice: A Mathematical Folktale* (Scholastic, 1997). The story illustrates the doubling "trick" but with rice instead of pennies.

Penny Doubling

Hold out a penny and tell a friend that by doubling this one penny you could become "filthy" rich in one month. Of course, your friend won't believe you. Get out a piece of paper and a pencil and prove it.

Day 1	$0.01	Day 2	$0.02	Day 3	$0.04
Day 4	$0.08	Day 5	$0.16	Day 6	$0.32
Day 7	$0.64	Day 8	$1.28	Day 9	$2.56
Day 10	$5.12	Day 11	$10.24	Day 12	$20.48
Day 13	$40.96	Day 14	$81.92	Day 15	$163.84

I'll stop here. You're probably saying this is nuts. Half of the month is gone and we only have $163.84. That's not exactly filthy rich! Well, continue with the doubling, by the end of thirty days you should have $5,368,709.12! Try it and see! You really COULD become rich, if only you could find someone to double your pennies for you!

• • •

Say I have $1 made up of fifty coins in my pocket. What denominations and how many of each do I have?

In my other pocket I have one hundred coins making a total of $5. What denominations and how many of each do I have?

Answer: Two dimes (twenty cents), **eight nickels** (forty cents), and **forty pennies** (forty cents).

Answer: There are several answers to this puzzle. I'll give you one: Five quarters ($1.25), **twenty dimes** ($2), **twenty-five nickels** ($1.25), and **fifty pennies** (fifty cents). See if you can figure out another answer.

Chapter 5
America's Bank—the Fed

The Federal Reserve System, also known as the Fed, was set up in 1913 by an act of Congress. Congress passed along its **constitutional right** "to coin money, and to regulate the value thereof," to the Fed.

The Fed acts as the central bank of the United States. Its activities are separate from the **U.S. Treasury**. Twelve Federal Reserve Districts and a Board of Governors based in Washington, D.C., make up the Federal Reserve System. Within the twelve Federal Reserve Districts are twelve regional banks with twenty-five branches. So, although the Fed acts as a central bank, its activities take place all around the United States.

The Fed is the bank that the federal government uses to pays its bills. For example, if your grandparents get social security checks from the government each month, these checks represent money in the Treasury account at the Federal Reserve Bank.

What else does the Fed do? Lots! Let's take a look at some of the Fed's functions:

- The Fed distributes newly minted and printed currency to banks that have accounts with the Federal Reserve. These banks are known as depository institutions.
- The money that the Federal Reserve banks receive from depository institutions is checked for condition. If bills are worn and torn, the Fed destroys them by shredding. If counterfeit bills are found, they are stamped

FUN FACT

Section eight of the Constitution not only grants Congress the right to coin money, it also gives Congress the "power to define and punish piracies and felonies committed on the high seas." Perhaps the signers of the Constitution were remembering Bartholomew Roberts, a pirate who in four years time captured more than four hundred ships! Roberts and other pirates were partly responsible for the lack of currency available to the colonies!

$ $ $

The Fed does not receive its operating money from taxes. Through its banking services such as check clearing, the Fed makes enough money to pay its own expenses.

WORDS to KNOW

Constitutional right— something that is granted by the U.S Constitution to the government or the individual.

"counterfeit" and sent to the U.S. Secret Service for investigation. Coins that are badly worn or bent are removed, as are foreign coins. The Fed advises the U.S. Treasury when more currency needs to be minted or printed to replace damaged currency.

- The Fed regulates; that is, it makes up rules for banks to follow in conducting business.

- Every day millions of payments, both by check and through electronic funds transfer, are handled by Federal Reserve Banks. Non-Federal-Reserve banks can buy check clearing services from the Fed rather than going to other check clearing-houses.

- If a bank has need of money and it cannot borrow from another non-Federal-Reserve bank, then the Fed is set up to loan the needed money. The Fed is known as "the lender of last resort." The interest the Fed charges is known as the "discount rate" because the Fed rate is usually less than the rate a bank can get from another lender.

- Perhaps most importantly, the Fed carries out the government's monetary policy. It controls the flow of money in three ways:

  1. The Fed requires banks to keep a certain amount of money in "reserve." By reserve is meant money that can't be used in loans and investments. By requiring banks to keep money in reserve, the Fed is able to make sure the economy stays balanced. If more money is needed in the economy, the Fed lowers the reserve requirements and banks can lend and invest more money. More money flows through the system. By raising the reserve requirement, the Fed decreases the flow of money.

  2. The Fed changes the interest rate that it charges to those banks borrowing money from the Fed. By

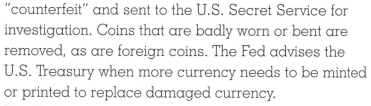

It was once believed that if a money spider walked on you, it meant that you would be coming into money! You'd better think twice before stepping on a spider!

WORDS to KNOW

U.S. Treasury—a governmental department responsible for the finances of the United States. The Treasury Department collects money due to the United States and pays all bills of the United States. The following are only a few of the bureaus that are a part of the U.S. Treasury: the Bureau of Engraving and Printing (produces paper money and postage stamps); the U.S. Mint (mints coins); the Internal Revenue Service (collects taxes); the U.S. Customs Service (collects taxes, called duties, on goods imported into the United States); and the U.S. Secret Service (investigates counterfeiters and smugglers as well as protects the president).

FUN FACT

Bank Tour

The twelve regional banks are located in Boston, New York, Philadelphia, Cleveland, Richmond, Atlanta, Chicago, St. Louis, Minneapolis, Kansas City, Dallas, and San Francisco. If you are located near any of these cities, you may be able to attend a tour of the bank, or an educational lecture on topics like "Currency and Counterfeits," "Money in Colonial New England," and "Basic Banking."

$ $ $

Did you know the average life of a $1 bill is eighteen months? The life of a $50 or a $100 bill is nine years! The New York Federal Reserve Bank destroys more than five million notes (bills) a day, and there are eleven other Federal Reserve Banks also shredding bills at the same time! Federal Reserve banks use high-speed processing machines that can go through seventy thousand bills per hour. Each bill is counted, its denomination and genuineness is confirmed, its condition determined, and it is bundled into a package! Not all shredded currency ends up in landfills. Some of it is recycled into products such as insulation and stationery.

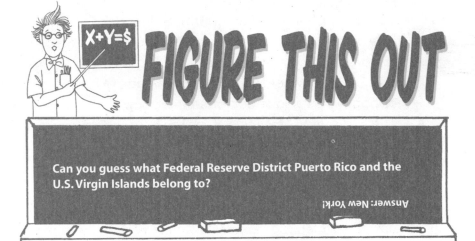

FIGURE THIS OUT

Can you guess what Federal Reserve District Puerto Rico and the U.S. Virgin Islands belong to?

Answer: New York!

charging higher interest rates, the borrowing banks in turn charge higher interest rates to their customers. Higher interest rates means less money will be borrowed because it costs more and the economy will slow down. Lowering the interest rate means more money will end up in circulation.

3. The Fed also affects the economy by buying and selling government securities. This activity is known as "open market operations." Securities are bonds or notes. By buying securities, the Fed is putting more money into the economy. By selling, the Fed is pulling money out of the economy.

• The Federal Reserve Bank in New York has a special role. It acts as fiscal agent in the United States for foreign central banks. That is, it arranges for financial transactions such as the purchase and sale of securities. It also stores, in its vaults, over $775 billion in currency, securities, and gold for foreign accounts, and foreign central banks and governments!

Money Move Challenge 1

What you need:
  Six pennies
  Six nickels

What you do:
1. Arrange the coins in a circle as shown.

2. Move the coins one at a time so that they end up in a circle of alternating coins (penny, nickel, penny, and so on).

3. A coin may be moved into the X in the middle, it may be moved into an empty spot next to it, or it may jump over one coin next to it to get into an empty space.

   You should be able to alternate the coins in less than fifteen moves!

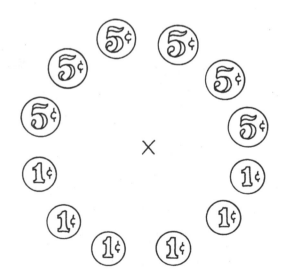

Money Move Challenge 2

What you need:
    Paper and pencil
    Three pennies
    Three nickels

What you do:
1. Draw a playing board with seven squares as shown. Arrange the coins as shown (start).

2. You need to end up with the coins in the finish position. Move one coin at a time. You may jump over a coin into an empty space. Pennies may be moved only to the right. Nickels may be moved only to the left.

4. You should be able to meet the challenge in fifteen moves!

START | 1¢ | 1¢ | 1¢ | | 5¢ | 5¢ | 5¢ |

FINISH | 5¢ | 5¢ | 5¢ | | 1¢ | 1¢ | 1¢ |

Chapter 6
Money for the New Millennium

As we enter the new millennium, changes in the way the world deals with money are being made. We'll look at the euro and the smart card as two of the changes already in progress.

THE EURO AND EUROLAND (NO, IT'S NOT A DISNEY THEME PARK!)

Imagine that you live in France. On the night of December 31, 1998 you went to bed with 100,000 francs in the bank. You wake up the next morning, January 1, 1999, and your 100,000 francs has turned into 655,957 euros! Is it magic? No, it's the future money of Europe!

Eleven European countries, with a population totaling 290 million, have banded together to form a single-currency zone. These countries are known as Euroland.

The eleven countries, Austria, Belgium, Finland, France, Germany, Ireland, Italy, Luxembourg, the Netherlands (Holland), Portugal, and Spain, are part of the European Union (EU). Four other European Union countries, Denmark, Greece, the United Kingdom, and Sweden, have not become part of Euroland.

So why did eleven countries give up their individual currencies for the euro? The euro will provide them with greater **economic** security and greater power on the economic world stage. For the average citizen of these countries, it will mean being able to travel from member country to member country

FUN FACT

The United States is a single-currency zone made up of 268 million people in fifty states.

Money ONLINE

Everything Kids'

http://

Say you're going to Euroland for a vacation. You can find out how much your $100 spending money is worth in euros by going to a currency conversion Web site such as *www.xe.net/ucc*. You can also find out how much your dollars are worth in Bulgarian lev, Greek drachmas, or Polish zloty!

Symbolism

The sign symbol for the U.S. dollar is a **$**. The British pound is designated by **£**. The euro has its own sign symbol, **€**. Not so coincidentally, the **€** looks like the capital letter E, the first letter in Euroland.

without having to deal with different money. The euro in France is the same as the euro in the Netherlands or Ireland or Italy.

What does the euro look like? Right now, it doesn't look like anything! For a period of time, January 1, 1999 through January 1, 2002, the euro only exists as "written money." That is, it is not something that you can hold in your hand. It's money in cyberspace! The flow of euro money through checks, bank transfers, and credit cards is done through computerized accounts—no cash is exchanged. If you get a printout of the accounts the money shows up as "written money."

Euroland citizens will need time to learn the new money. A conversion rate has been set up to ease the transition. For example, one euro is equal to 6.55957 French francs. If you were in Germany, one euro is equal to 1.95583 marks. These rates will remain the same until 2002. By that time, Euroland citizens should be thinking in terms of the euro!

While the euro is "written money," Euroland countries will continue to use their old coins and paper money for everyday business. Starting January 1, 2002, euro notes and coins will be

FUN FACT

The design of the euro notes is the result of a competition held during 1996. Surveys were made of over two thousand taxi drivers, bank tellers, and sales people in determining the winner. Robert Kalina of Austria designed the winning images to be used on the seven denominations. For a look at Kalina's designs, go to the Web site at *www.ecb.int/emi/about/about06.htm*.

Money ONLINE $

Everything Kids'

Back | Forward

http://

View the euro coins from this Web site:
http://pacific.commerce.ubc.ca/xr/euro/

made available. There may be a short time when both the new notes and coins and the old-style moneys are being used, but, this can go on only until July 1, 2002. On that date, the euro will be the only money accepted as legal tender. Does it all sound confusing? You bet it is!

Euro notes will come in denominations of 5, 10, 20, 50, 100, 200, and 500 and will be in different sizes and colors. The fronts of the notes will have images of windows and gateways. These are not pictures from any particular country, but represent a "spirit of openness and cooperation" between the members of the EU. Also on the front of each note is a circle of golden stars against a blue background.

QUIZ

In all, the euro is replacing eleven different currencies. Can you match up these eight Euroland countries with the names of their "old" money?

Country

1. Belgium
2. Austria
3. Portugal
4. Italy
5. the Netherlands
6. Ireland
7. Spain
8. Finland

Currency

A. Pesata
B. Lira
C. Punt
D. Guilder
E. Schilling
F. Escudo
G. Markka
H. Franc

Answers: 1(H); 2(E); 3(F); 4(B); 5(D); 6(C); 7(A); 8(G)

Pictures of fictional bridges, along with a map of Europe, are found on the backs of the notes.

All the notes are produced by the European Central Bank, headquartered in Frankfurt, Germany. The European Central Bank is similar in some ways to our Federal Reserve System. The euro notes will have advanced security features to guard against counterfeiting.

There are several billion coins currently in circulation in the EU. It is a massive undertaking to replace them with euro coins by the year 2002. Euro coins will be minted in individual Euroland countries, not the European Central Bank. There will be 1, 2, 5, 10, 20, and 50 cent coins, plus 1 and 2 euro coins. One hundred cents will equal one euro.

Eight denominations interpreted by eleven countries will result in a total of eighty-eight different coins! The obverse will have a common EU design of a map of Europe against a background of lines attached to the twelve stars of the European

Plastics!

Who knows, one day U.S. paper money may be made of plastic. It already is in Australia! Plastic bills will last longer, but as a friend living in Sydney told me, "We just have to make sure the pockets are empty before we iron the clothes!"

Money ONLINE

Everything Kids'

Back Forward

http://

The Internet has rapidly become a part of our lives—ads on television list Web sites; so do highway billboards. People buy and sell online. E-commerce is now an accepted way of doing business. You had to know that someone would come up with e-cash! For a look at one company's experiment with e-cash visit this Web site: *www.ecashtechnologies.com.*

flag. The reverse side will display national symbols of the origi-nating country's choice. All the euro coins, no matter what the country of origin, will be accepted as payment in every Euroland country.

SMART CARDS

So what is a smart card? A smart card looks like a regular plastic credit card, but with one difference; it has a computer in it—a tiny computer run by an even tinier battery!

How is it changing money? It moves us closer to becoming a cashless society— society that no longer uses coins and bills to transact its business.

A smart card is like having your bank account in your hand. If you need to buy something, you hand over your smart card and the price of whatever it is you are paying for is automati-cally subtracted from the money in your account.

Smart cards will also be multi-functional; that is, they will be used for purposes other than banking. Medical information may be stored on a smart card, or your smart card may allow you to get into secure (locked) buildings for which you need a special code that is on your smart card. Smart cards are cur-rently being used on college campuses with great success.

Chances are good you haven't yet seen a smart card. But there's a "Smart Card Museum" online already! The cyber-museum traces the history of the smart card. Visit it at *www.cardshow.com/museum/welcome.html*.

None in a Row Challenge

What you need:
Four pennies
Three nickels
Three dimes
Three quarters
Three half-dollars (dollar coins may be used,
    or if you can't find any of these
      larger denomination coins, use buttons!)
Paper and pencil
Ruler

What you do:
1. Using the ruler, measure a square eight inches by eight inches on the paper. Make a mark every two inches.

2. Make a grid with sixteen squares as shown.

3. Place all the coins on the grid so that there are no coins of the same denomination on any one line. That includes diagonals too!

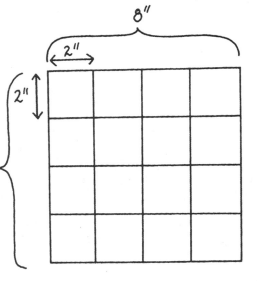

The Don't Tricks

DON'T MOVE THE PENNIES!
Here is your challenge—remove the dollar bill without moving the pennies.

What you need:
> A soda bottle with a flat cap. A full bottle is better because it won't tip over.
> A dollar bill
> Five pennies

What you do:
1. Arrange the coins and the bill on top of the bottle as shown.

2. Remove the bill without moving or touching the pennies.

3. After you've tried it a couple of times, look below for the answer to how it's done.

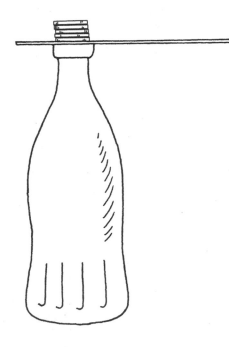

How it's done:
Holding the end of the bill straight out with one hand, execute a "karate chop" with the index finger of your other hand. Aim for George Washington's face! If you do the chop quickly enough, the bill will slide out and the pennies will remain undisturbed on top of the bottle!

The Don't Tricks

DON'T TIP THE BOTTLE

What you need:
   One soda bottle
   A dollar bill

What you do:
1. Place the bottle upside down on the bill as shown.
2. Remove the bill without touching or tipping the bottle.

How it's done:
   Start rolling up the bill as shown, being careful to keep your fingers away from the bottle. If you roll the bill slowly and tightly, you should be able to roll it out from under the bottle without tipping it over!

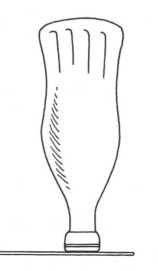
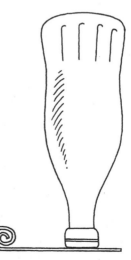

Chapter 7
Money—How to Get It and What to Do with It

You already know money doesn't grow on trees. You can't pick it, so how do you, a kid, get it? There are several ways:

- You can receive an allowance.
- You can weasel it out of your parents ("C'mon, Dad, I need some money, I'm the only kid in school who doesn't have _____." (You fill in the blank).
- You can get money as a gift from family or friends.
- You can earn it by doing manual labor, performing a service, or selling something.
- You can invest money to make money.

Ashley S., age 13, of Prince George, British Columbia offered this advice, "Make sure you don't waste your money on something you want now but won't care about later."

ALLOWANCES

Many kids receive an allowance from their parents. An allowance is, quite simply, an amount of money given on a regular basis—in most cases, weekly.

If you do not get an allowance, you can probably convince your parents to give you one. Your parents believe in education, right? Well, working with an allowance teaches kids responsibility and the value of money.

Many parents are afraid that kids will not spend their allowance wisely. You may make some foolish spending choices, but if you do, the decision to do so was your own, and hopefully you will learn from your mistakes. Much of learning occurs through trial and error—ask any scientist!

Explain to your parents that money is something you will have to deal with for the rest of your life. It is better that you make your mistakes early on than later when the stakes may be higher! Explain that you will have a family some day, and

FUN FACT

Allowances

Zillions, the consumer advice magazine for kids, recently did a national survey on allowances. The results appeared in the January/February 1999 issue. Check it out at your local public library and see what the 1,059 kids who were surveyed had to say about the money they receive from their parents.

Money ONLINE

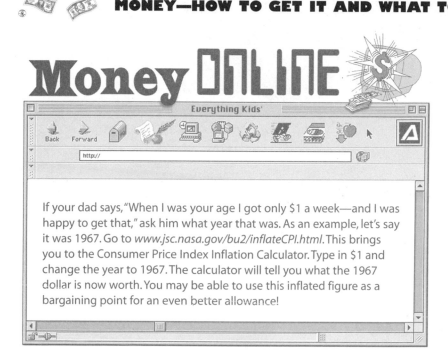

Everything Kids'

If your dad says, "When I was your age I got only $1 a week—and I was happy to get that," ask him what year that was. As an example, let's say it was 1967. Go to *www.jsc.nasa.gov/bu2/inflateCPI.html*. This brings you to the Consumer Price Index Inflation Calculator. Type in $1 and change the year to 1967. The calculator will tell you what the 1967 dollar is now worth. You may be able to use this inflated figure as a bargaining point for an even better allowance!

"A single penny fairly got is worth a thousand that are not."
—*German proverb*

you need to know how to manage your money. Not everything is taught at school!

How much should you get? That all depends on your family circumstances, but perhaps a good negotiating point would be to suggest $1 for every year of age. For example, if you are eight, you would get $8 a week. If you are 14, you would get $14.

Rather than pick an amount out of a hat, why not do a study. Spend a week or two and write down everything you buy for yourself and everything that is bought for you by your parents. Leave nothing off your list—write down the twenty-five cents you put in the gum machine at the grocery store, the money you spend for lunch at school, the $15 your mom coughs up for your karate lessons, the cost of a new pen and some notebook paper. Don't forget to include the money you put into the church collection basket or the money you used to buy your friend a birthday present.

FUN FACT

In the *Zillions* survey, 43 percent of the kids interviewed said they received an allowance—31 percent said they got neither an allowance nor spending money! More than eight out of ten kids in the survey said, "all kids should get an allowance." What do you think?

At the end of the week, total up the costs. Has it been a typical week? Will your expenses be roughly the same from week to week?

Go over the list with your parents. Perhaps you can deduct the cost of school lunches from your weekly expenses. But, you should keep the cost of the popsicle you get on the way home from school. Decide what expenses are your parents' responsibility and what are yours. Consider building in an additional amount for savings. Is the amount you need met by the dollar-for-each-year-of-age formula suggested earlier? If not, what would be a good figure? Discuss it with your parents.

Another way to negotiate allowances is to discuss chores. Here again, it helps to make up a chart of a week's worth of chores. A simple chart would have the days of the week across the top. Under each day, list the chores you have done. Do you put out the trash three times a week? Then under Monday, Wednesday, and Friday, write in "put out trash." If you set the

FUN FACT

According to a survey reported in the September/October 1999 issue of *Zillions*, the number one thing kids spend their money on is snacks! They spend about $5 a week on them!

Charting Your Allowance

Here's how Justin W.'s family handles the issue: "Sometimes my Mom doesn't have the cash, so we have a chart on the kitchen wall that tells how much money I have. If I'm in a store and I want to buy something she pays for it and I subtract it from the chart."

Everything Kids'

http://

A great Web site to visit if you and your parents need advice on allowances is *http://pages.prodigy.com/kidsmoney/alllist.htm*.

Read All About It!

In *The Kids' Allowance Book* by Amy Nathan (Walker and Co., 1998) 166 kids, the "Allowance All-Star Squad," and their parents discuss allowances and the pluses and minuses of their individual arrangements.

> "Money buys everything except brains."
> —*Yiddish proverb*

table for dinner every day, write it in every day. Do you mow the lawn or shovel the driveway? Then list these things as seasonal tasks at the bottom of the page so that they may be used to get a total picture of what you do. After the week is up, you and your parents can look at the list. They may be surprised to see how much you really do around the house, or you may be embarrassed at how little you do!

In any case, you and your parents need to decide which of those things are just "good family member" chores and which are a little extra and deserve an allowance. It could be doing the dishes every day and feeding the cats, even if you hate the cats! Or, your parents may decide just to give you the money!

Are there any other strings attached to your allowance? Probably. Once you start on an allowance you may have to pay for all your expenses—that is, you don't get extra money to go to a movie or a concert. If you can't pay for it out of your allowance or your savings, you don't go. So if it's the first of the month and you and your friends have big plans to

> "I still get my allowance if I am sick or away at science camp and can't do my chores," Tyler S. told me.

FUN FACT

A Third or a Quarter

One of these two arrangements might work in your household. The "one-third" rule: one-third to spend, one-third to share (gifts, donations to charity, etc.), and one-third to save. The "one-quarter" plan: one-fourth to spend, one-fourth to share, one-fourth to save, and one-fourth to invest for the future. Discusss all your options, one of which may be your parents telling you, "It's your money, do with it what you want!"

FUN FACT

Family Matters

Kids need to be aware of their parents' needs also. There may come a time when your parents are unable to regularly pay you your allowance—perhaps your dad loses his job, or your elderly grandmother requires expensive care. Your parents will appreciate the fact that you can understand their situation and not nag. Remember, a family works together.

Brand Names Tradeoff

Your parents are expected to feed and clothe you, but at your age, you may no longer need them to do the actual purchasing. Try setting up a clothing allowance in addition to your regular allowance. This money is to be spent only for clothing. It may be an eye-opener for you. When you have to hand over the money for your own jeans, you may leave the brand names behind and look for the equally durable store brand. Buying the brand name jeans may mean your holey socks will have to last until your next clothing allowance payment!

Money ONLINE

Everything Kids'

http://

Rosemary E. of S. Berwick, Maine, told me, "I think it's a good idea to give some of your money to a charity." But, she also wanted to know, "What charities put the most amount of your money into programs to help people?" That's a good question! Visit the National Charities Information Bureau at *www.give.org* to check on over four hundred national charitable organizations.

attend the opening of a new movie three weeks from now, start saving part or all of your allowance for your ticket (and some popcorn, of course)!

Some parents feel that putting part of the allowance money into savings or investments will encourage setting long-term goals. It won't be long before you're looking at colleges! So, you may be required to put "untouchable" money in the bank every week.

Will you receive cash, or a check that will require you to go to the bank each week? Will your parents hold onto your allowance money for you? Then how will you get it if you need it? Again, talk it over.

If you and your parents want to be satisfied with your plan, then it is important that you all come to an agreement beforehand about what is expected. Put in writing what you will receive each week, on what day you will receive it, and what you are responsible for doing. You may even wish to put in a paragraph stating that the agreement is subject to renegotiation in six months or a year. If both you and your parents sign

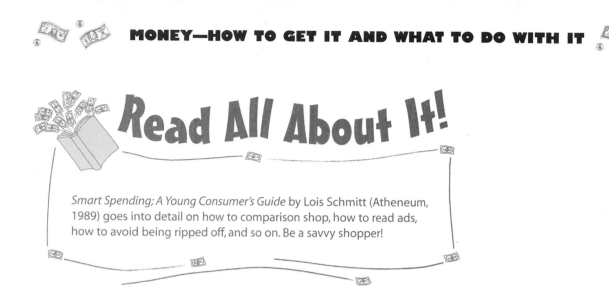

Read All About It!

Smart Spending; A Young Consumer's Guide by Lois Schmitt (Atheneum, 1989) goes into detail on how to comparison shop, how to read ads, how to avoid being ripped off, and so on. Be a savvy shopper!

the agreement, you have made a contract—just like in the real world of business!

Although we've been talking about weekly allowances, there are other arrangements that can be made. If your mom or dad gets paid once every two weeks, then it might make sense for you to be paid on the same basis. Some kids are paid monthly to give them practice in setting up and living within a budget.

GIFTS OF MONEY

As you get older, relatives have a harder time figuring out what to get you for your birthday or for the holidays. Sometimes an aunt will get you the same thing year after year after year. Just because you liked the fake-fur bear slippers she got you when you were four, she thinks you will still like them when you are fourteen.

A gift of money is always appreciated by kids, but many grownups don't like to give money for fear it will be frittered away.

Here's what you can do. Is there something that you need to save for? A CD player?

Spending Habits

If you find yourself wondering, "Where did it all go?" then perhaps it's time to keep track of your spending. Go back to listing all the expenses you had over a week's time. Once you see where it has all gone, you can rethink your spending habits!

Money ONLINE

Everything Kids'

Back | Forward

http://

How much will it cost you to go to college when you get out of high school? The "Education Calculator" at *www.cunamutual.com/realwrld/educcalc.htm* can help you figure it out.

$ $ $

The Internet is a good place to comparison shop. The Web site *www.pricescan.com* is a service that allows you to compare the price for an item, such as a computer game, at several Internet sites. Remember, although the prices for items bought online may be good, you still have to consider the costs of shipping and handling. If you add in shipping and handling, it may end up costing more than it would to buy the item at your local discount store. But, you won't know until you do the research!

Spending money for two weeks at soccer camp?

Do some consumer homework. Figure out how much you will need. How long will you have to save? When is the camp payment due? If you want the CD player, check out a consumer magazine such as *Consumer Reports* for reliability ratings. Read the Sunday ads for sale prices. Learn how to comparison shop. Ask your friends if they are happy with the CD players they have. Listen when they tell you that the sound of the XYZ brand player isn't good, or that you'll have to replace the batteries every ten hours with the ABC brand player. Check out the price of batteries while you're at it! Decide upon the best CD player for you. How much will it cost? How much do you already have? How much more do you need?

Tell the gift givers about your plans. Maybe if your aunt knows what a mature shopper you are, she might want to help you out with something green for your well-thought-out purchase, rather than something fuzzy for your feet!

Money gifts for college are frequently given to an older kid. Since you have several years before you're ready to attend college, you can put these gifts into an Education IRA or save them until you have enough for a certificate of deposit—see Chapter 4.

Investing the "for college" gift money is another option, but with investment comes risk. We'll discuss investing later in Chapter 9.

Fun with Money

Money Tricks

TOGETHERNESS

This is a trick that looks amazing and is simple to do too!

What you need:
    Two small metal paper clips
    A dollar bill

What you do:
1. Loosely fold the bill into thirds and place the paper clips at the top as shown.

2. Take the bill in two hands and quickly pull the ends outward. The paper clips will fly off the bill and will be clipped together!

How it's done:
    By pulling on the ends, the two clips are forced together and interlock.

Fun with Money

HIDING A COIN
Coin tricks have been around probably as long as there have been coins. Everyone has seen a magician pull a coin out of somebody's ear. Wouldn't you like to be able to do it too?

What you need:
One coin (contrary to what you'd think, it should be a large coin rather than a small one)

What you do:
Method 1
1. Hold your hand palm side to the audience. It seems to be totally empty, but a coin is being held between your first and second finger, sticking out the back.

2. Bring your fingers inward and use your thumb to make the coin "appear."

Method 2
1. Hold your hand open with the back facing your audience. Use the fleshy part under your thumb to hold the coin.
2. Practice, practice, practice! By "palming" the coin this way, you should be able to make a coin appear from someone's ear or nose.

Read All About It!

If you get really good at this simple "magic" trick, look in your local library for other magic books. Want to specialize in coin tricks? Look for *Coin Magic* (Klutz Press, 1997). It's nothing but coin tricks!

Chapter 8
Earning Money

An allowance or gifts may provide you with money enough for your day-to-day expenses, but what if you want to buy something special? Perhaps a pair of cross-country skis, or an acoustic guitar.

You'll need to make money, but how? Look at the chores you do. Is there something that needs to be done around the house or yard that doesn't fall into the category of required chores?

Perhaps your parents want to paint the hallway. You could do the job of removing the wallpaper, washing the walls, taping off the trim, and so on. Discuss with your parents what would be a fair wage for the job, then offer to do it. If they agree, decide upon a time for you to do the work. If your dad plans on painting on Sunday, promise to do the prep work Saturday afternoon, even if it means giving up a trip to the mall with your friends.

How else can you earn money? Get a job! Fast food restaurants are often the first place a kid gets a regular job. Malls are also good places to look for a first job.

Are you at least fourteen years old? If not, then getting a "regular" job may not be possible. Many states require that you be fourteen unless you work on the family farm. How can you find out about the rules in your state? A school guidance counselor will be able to help you. He or she can tell you about working papers, the number of hours you are allowed to work per week during the school year, and so on. Child labor laws regulate the work young people can do, to ensure they stay healthy and get a good education.

FUN FACT

Too Good to Be True

You've seen the flyers attached to telephone poles, or you've seen ads in the newspaper that say, "Make hundreds of dollars a week at home. No experience needed!" Sounds too good to be true, right? Right you are! It's a scam. Someone is trying to swindle you. If you answer the ad you will be asked to send money to receive the instructions on how you too can make hundreds. If you send the money, you'll receive a photocopied sheet telling you to make up flyers, attach them to telephone poles, and then wait for suckers like yourself to send you money! If you follow the instructions, you'll end up spending money making photocopies, but it is doubtful if you'll make it back! Variations on the scam involve stuffing envelopes at home. Again, you'll have to spend money, but you probably won't make any.

Refund?

If you have taxes "withheld," (that is, taken out) from your paycheck, you should fill out a federal income tax form. In many cases, a kid can get back (a "refund") the full amount!

Many years ago in China, coins came on a money tree! The coins were attached to metal "branches" and were broken off and used as needed.

What are some jobs you can get without having to get working papers? Babysitting, house cleaning, and yard work are three that are popular with kids. Others include washing cars (great for groups that need to make money!), newspaper delivery, dog walking, or pet sitting.

Look into babysitting courses offered by the local American Red Cross chapter, the YMCA, your county extension, or the local recreation department. Parents will appreciate the fact that you have been trained, and you will be better prepared for emergencies. Kids who are not old enough to babysit can become "mother's helpers." A helper entertains the children so that the mom can get some housework done! Babysitting is not just for girls! Mothers love to hire older boys to babysit.

Yardwork, or cleaning out garages and attics, is a great job for those who like physical activity. For jobs like these you may have to invest in some equipment such as rakes, shovels, and work gloves. Often though, the person hiring you will have the equipment, but not the time, for the job. A word of warning—never accept a job that would put you in danger, such as trimming branches near electrical lines.

Here are a few more jobs you may not have thought of:

- *Computer installation and instruction*—You could set up computers and printers for adults you know who've bought new computers but don't know the first thing about using them!
- *Web-page design*—Kids who know HTML (hypertext mark-up language) can help small businesses or organizations set up their Web sites.

Taxes, Taxes, Taxes

When you get a regular job and receive a paycheck, you'll have to pay income taxes. Taxes are a percentage of your pay that goes to the federal, state, and local governments. Besides income taxes, there are also sales taxes, real estate taxes, and other miscellaneous taxes.

It sounds unfair having to pay so many taxes, but when you take a minute to think about what tax dollars are used for, you may change your mind. Local governments use taxes to pay for schools—the salaries of teachers and the costs of constructing and taking care of the buildings. Taxes also pay for the textbooks, the basketballs, the art supplies, the school nurse, etc. And that's not all—local taxes pay for the police and fire departments. What pays for plowing the snow in the winter? Taxes. Taxes also put the chlorine in the public swimming pool each summer (and don't forget they pay for the lifeguards).

State taxes pay for health care and services for the poor, as well as state police, education, and roads.

Federal taxes pay for interstate highways, national parks, the military.... The list goes on and on! It's incredible, when you think about all that you get for your tax dollar!

Job Ideas

Rosemary E., who is 12, helps out at a B & B during the summer. (B & B stands for "bed and breakfast." It's a home business where people pay to stay overnight and have breakfast.) Rosemary lays out quilts, makes beds, washes dishes, and works in the garden for about $5.50 an hour.

The Going Rate

How much should a babysitter be paid? Becki D. of Chelmsford, Massachusetts makes $4 an hour. Valerie L. of Muskegon, Michigan gets between $2 and $5 an hour. Ask around to see what the "going rates" are in your town.

$ $ $

Ann Martin has made a fortune, not by babysitting, but by writing about babysitting! *The Baby-Sitters Club* series has more than one hundred titles, and was even made into a movie! Maybe someday you can write about your adventures as a babysitter!

- *Word-processing*—If you've grown up with a computer you've probably got keyboarding down pat!
- *Volunteer Positions*—Nonpaying jobs, such as volunteering at the animal shelter, are valuable for the experience you get. You learn to follow instructions, work according to a schedule, interact with the public, and so on. These are all skills that can later be applied to a paying job. And don't overlook the fact that if you prove yourself to be a good worker in a volunteer position, you may get first notice when a paying position opens up!

BE AN ENTREPRENEUR

Entrepreneur is a big word for someone who sets up a business. Have you considered starting up a business? Selling lemonade from the bottom of your driveway is a good start, but I'm talking about committing to a long-term plan and working hard to meet your goals.

First you start with an idea or an interest. Do you enjoy helping your mom plan for family parties? Shopping for matching paper plates and cups? Making up a menu of special treats? You might want to think about a party business and offer your service to other moms.

Expanding on the party idea, think about entertaining little kids at birthday parties. Would you like to clown around and get dressed up in

> "If a little money does not go out, great money will not come in."
> —*Chinese proverb*

costumes? Taking the idea one step further, how about making twisted balloon sculptures? Could you learn to make balloon animals and silly hats? All the little kids I know love to watch balloon animals being made. And, they love it even more if they get to take a balloon home!

So now you've got an idea. You can set up a business entertaining little kids at parties by making balloon animals. Next you need a plan—a business plan.

Read All About It!

Babysitting Resource

For more information on babysitting, look for one of these at your local public library: *The Babysitter's Handbook* by K. D. Kuch (Random House, 1997), *The Ultimate Baby-Sitter's Handbook*, by Debra Mostow Zakarin (Price Stern Sloan, Inc., 1997). The following site provides basics for new sitters: *www.kidshealth.org/teen/workplay/babysit.html*.

Consider your situation. Do you have the time to do all that is involved? Will it interfere with your schoolwork? Will your parents approve? Think about the balloon animal business. You'll need to learn special skills and practice your act. Should you make or buy a costume, or will a silly bow tie and a simple balloon hat be enough? How about a catchy name for your business? Where will you advertise your services? What will you charge your customers?

Before you start on any of these, you want to do a market survey. What's a market survey? It's a study that will tell you if there is a need for your business in the area you live. Wouldn't it be horrible if you spent time and money setting up your business and then found out that there are twenty other businesses in your town that entertain kids at birthday parties!

Start in your own neighborhood. Are there many kids ages eight and under? Ask the parents of these children if they ever hire entertainment for their kids' parties. Who have they hired? Were they happy with what they got? Would they be interested

What do you call a chicken that robs people?

A peck-pocket.

in balloon entertainment? What would they be willing to pay for someone to keep the kids amused for about forty-five minutes?

Get out the yellow pages. Look up clowns or parties and see if there are any listings for children's entertainment. Go to the public library. There may be a children services directory that lists entertainment services in your area. (If there is a directory, make a note of the publisher. If your business is a success you could advertise in the directory!)

Okay, your market survey has left you feeling that there's definitely a need in your town for your service. What's next?

Training. Having seen a balloon twister at work and thinking, "It looks easy enough," doesn't mean balloon twisting is easy! Again, go to the public library and look for books on balloons and/or clowning. Remember how the people you've seen making balloon animals always kept up a steady stream of talk (known as "patter")? Take out a few books on jokes.

You'll need start-up money to get your business going. You may have to buy a balloon twisting book if you can't find one at the library. Also necessary are a supply of balloons and perhaps a small pump if your lung power isn't great! Look at your own savings to see if you have enough. If not, discuss with your parents if they will loan you the money until your first paying "gig." To add a professional touch to your arrangement, put the

Read All About It!

Captain Visual's Big Book of Balloon Art! : A Complete Book of Balloonology for Beginners and Advanced Twisters (Citadel Press, 1995) has lots of fun ideas to keep your young audiences entertained! To buy the special balloons necessary, try a local party store, or www.clownsupplies.com.

> "…almost all dream analysts agree that finding money has to do with the dreamer's discovery of new and positive qualities and potentials within herself or himself."
> —From *In Your Dreams: Falling, Flying, and Other Dream Themes*

promise of repayment in writing. Your parents will realize that you are serious and may be more willing to help you.

While you're busy practicing, you can also be thinking about a name for your business. How does "Balloon Buddy" sound? Or, are you the "Balloon Guy?" Maybe you're a "Balloon Artist!" Ask your parents and friends what they think of your name choice.

After much practice you will be able to tell if this business idea will really work. If you feel confident enough to perform in front of an audience, try out your act on your relatives and friends first. Then you could volunteer at your local library or at a daycare center. If you do well, the parents of kids at the library will want to hire you for their kids' upcoming birthday parties.

At this point you will need to be ready to tell a potential customer your price. You got some ideas of what the market will "bear," that is, what people are willing to pay, from your market survey. A parent may help by telephoning a professional entertainer and asking for his or her rates. Since you are new at the business, you should be willing to be paid a whole lot less! Professional rates are something for you to shoot for—a business goal.

This might be a good time to talk about business goals. Entrepreneurs set goals for their businesses. Goals should be realistic. In the balloon twisting business it wouldn't do you any good to state your goal as, "to earn a million dollars in my first year." A more realistic goal would be, "book one party a month in my first year." This is a reachable goal.

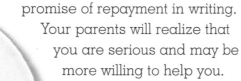

Tips for Success

Some tips for keeping your customers, the people buying your services, happy:

- *Be on time* and show up ready to work. Have your equipment with you, do not keep your customers waiting while you go home to get your grass clippers.
- *Be neat* in appearance and in your work. Don't forget to clean up after yourself when you finish the job, and put the customer's tools back where they belong.
- *Be complete.* Finish the job. Before you start, know exactly what the customer expects you to do. If your customer wanted you to mow the front and the back lawns, and you've only done the front, do you think you'll be hired again?
- *Be polite.* The customer will appreciate it if you say please and thank you. Look directly at the person you are speaking with. Never be rude!
- *Be safe.* Always go over safety procedures before starting a job. If you are babysitting, make sure you get the names and phone numbers of people to be contacted in case of emergency.

Business Start-up Steps

We've been going through the process of starting up a balloon business, but you can start almost any new business by following the same procedure:

- *Start with an idea.* Is there an activity or a product you enjoy? Make sure it's something you can continue to enjoy even after you've done it a hundred times!
- *Do a market survey.* Ask around to see who might be interested in your business or service. Do people eagerly await your services, or do they not understand or need what you are offering? Will your business have a chance of succeeding?
- *Have a business plan.* What do you need to do to get ready, and what will you need to do to stay in business?
- *Develop a mission statement and set goals.* What do you hope to accomplish?

Businesses also prepare mission statements—that is, a brief explanation of what they are trying to do. For the balloon business it could be something like, "to provide comical entertainment for children ages four to eight by making balloon animals." Try it—write a mission statement for whatever business you would consider starting up. If you cannot do it easily, then perhaps you don't really know what it is you are trying to do. You may need to rethink your business!

You're ready to go, right? Wrong! Have you thought about a contract? It's a business! You should spell out for your customers exactly what they will receive. A contract should include the date, start time and place, and how long the entertainment will last. Other agreed upon conditions like "each child in attendance will receive two animals" should be included. The price you are charging and how you expect payment, for example, "$25 cash or check on the day of performance" should be a part of your contract. You will also need to have a place where both you and the customer can sign and add the date.

Finally, the day arrives. You show up on time. You and the party kids have a good time. You get paid your $25. Now it's time to see if you've made any money. But, you say, "I just made $25." Yes, you did, but did you remember to subtract your expenses?

Here's the way it looks:

EXPENSES

$14.95	for balloon book
+ $5.75	for package of balloons for practice
+ $5.75	for balloons for the contracted date
= $26.45	Total Expenses
– $25.00	Income
= -$1.45	Loss

If you subtract your expenses from your income, you find that you made -$1.45 for your first gig! A negative amount is known as a loss.

Have you failed? No, of course not. You did a good job. Two mothers asked for your flyer (you did remember to make one up before your performance, didn't you?), and a dad booked you on the spot! Give yourself a pat on the back!

The second gig is easier. You have a larger audience this time, so you have to buy more balloons, but you don't have to buy another book! You get paid $25. Now have you made money? Let's see.

When Thomas Edison was asked how it felt to fail 1,000 times before he was finally able to produce the light bulb, he said, "I didn't fail 1,000 times. The light bulb was an invention with 1,001 steps." Edison had a winning attitude!

EXPENSES

$5.75	additional balloons	$25.00	Income
+ $1.00	copying costs for flyers	– $10.05	Expenses
+ $3.30	cost for mailing 10 flyers	= $14.95	Profit
= $10.05	Total Expenses		

This time when you subtract your expenses from your income you find that you made $14.95! A profit!

Your business has begun. Now you should update your business plan so that you can continue in business. Include advertising, continued training (you have to keep wowing your customers by twisting new animals), setting up a system of **bookkeeping,** paying taxes, and seeking free publicity. If you do a free show, ask the group you do it for to invite the local newspaper. You'll get your picture in the paper and will make yourself known to more potential customers. And if you get a few parties signed up in advance, you may be able to buy your balloons in a larger quantity so they'll cost you less per balloon.

Flyers are a great form of advertising for a young entrepreneur. You can easily design one on a computer if you're not artistically inclined. Make copies on colored paper. Brightly colored flyers attract attention on bulletin boards. Ask to post your flyers on bulletin boards at the public library, your school, your church, the grocery store, and the town recreation department. Make sure you put in your telephone number so that a customer can get in touch with you! Don't put your rate on the flyer. This allows you room to negotiate. You may be willing to charge the Daisy Girl Scouts less, or nothing at all, if it means more people (potential customers) will see you perform. You'll also feel good about doing a charitable deed.

The best form of advertising is free—word of mouth. If you do a good job, and someone recommends you to another person who's looking for your type of service, then you've been given free promotion! If customers tell you you've done a good job, ask if you may use them as a reference. A reference is another person's word that you can do the job well.

WORDS to KNOW

Bookkeeping—is keeping a record of business accounts and transactions. A simple system would involve keeping track of business expenses (these amounts are known as debits) and income (known as credits). You must begin your books with a dollar amount known as the starting balance. During a period you record all the income and expenses. You may decide to do your books on a weekly, monthly, quarterly (3 months), semi-annual, or annual basis. One word of caution, the longer you wait, the harder it becomes to keep track of things! At the end of the period, you subtract all the debit amounts and add all the credit amounts to get your ending balance. For the next period, the ending balance becomes the new starting balance.

Why did Robin Hood steal from the rich?

Because the poor have no money.

Money ONLINE

Everything Kids'

http://

The "Piggy Bank Info Exchange" at
http://members.aol.com/fpanettier/index.html has pictures of
hundreds of piggy banks!
    The "First Worldwide Piggy Band Home Page" at
www.geocities.com/Paris/9896/ has pictures and a whole lot of
links—and I'm not talking about sausage!

After a period of about six months, sit down and evaluate your business. Is it going according to your expectations? Are you happy doing the work? Do your losses outnumber your profits? Are you keeping up with your school work? Your social life?

At this point you may decide to throw in the towel and quit. You've given it your best, so there is nothing to be sorry about. In the adult world, 70 to 80 percent of new businesses do not make it beyond the first year!

If you are enjoying your work, meeting new people, and making a little money then you may decide to keep going. Good for you! Or, maybe you've been successful but you've outgrown your business idea and would like to do some other business.

Either way, setting up a business has been a valuable learning experience—you learned a skill, you increased your self-confidence, and you proved to your parents that you can see a project through.

FUN FACT

Everyone has heard of a piggy bank. Why do we have piggy banks and not doggy banks, or fishy banks? Good question! The term piggy comes from a reddish type of clay used for making pottery in the Middle Ages, *pygg*. Often money was kept in a pot (jar) made of pygg. Over the years, pygg pottery became known as piggery. A piggery is also a place where pigs are kept. Pygg and pig got all mixed up. One thing lead to another and by the eighteenth century people were making pig-shaped banks!

MORE WAYS TO MAKE MONEY

Here are a few more ways to make some money:

1. Have a yard sale. Ask your family to help gather up all the things they no longer need. Clean out your closets and the basement. Gather together the soccer shoes that are two sizes too small and the ice skates that both you and your younger siblings have outgrown. Wash those sweaters, and clean out the hamster cage that's been sitting in the garage since Fluffy died. Invite the neighbors to join you in a street-wide yard sale. Post notices and put an ad in the local paper, then pray it doesn't rain!

2. If your parents don't already do it, clip coupons from the flyers in the Sunday paper. Ask ahead of time if your parents will be willing to give you the money they save on the grocery bill by using the coupons—or maybe they'll give you half, so you both save! I've found that if you alphabetize your coupons by product name, it makes it easier to find the coupon you need at checkout. While you unpack the groceries, think about how fifty cents here and thirty-five cents there added up to $3.75 in savings!

3. Many stores have boards near the exits that hold rebate offers. A rebate is a return of part of the purchase price of an item. Check the boards after you've done your shopping to see if there is a rebate offer. If there is,

> "Wealth is like seawater; the more we drink, the thirstier we become."
> —*Arthur Schopenhauer*

FUN FACT

DJ W. of Greensburg, Indiana said he can count on getting $2 every time he takes cans to the recycling center!

$ $ $

Are you interested in how far a dollar bill travels? If so, visit *www.wheresgeorge.com*. You enter the series (year) and serial number of a dollar bill, and your zip code. If the dollar bill has been entered before, you will get a list of all the cities and states where that bill has been. If your dollar bill has not been entered before, it will begin to be tracked. You mark the bill with the Web address and send it on its way by spending it! Check the site often to see where your bill has been.

follow the directions on the form and wait for your check to arrive in the mail!

4. Recycle old newspapers and aluminum cans. You can make money and feel good about saving the environment!

Whether you babysit, rake leaves, or clip coupons, the important thing to remember about earning money is to find something you like to do. There is a proverb that goes, "He who likes his work, to him work comes easy."

Money Science

With these activities you can play around and be learning science at the same time.

PENNY TOWERS

What you need:
    Thirty pennies (if you get good you may need more!)

What you do:
1. On a flat surface, start by placing one penny on top of another. How many pennies can you stack before your tower topples?
2. Start again, only this time, push the second coin just slightly off center. Add another penny in the same way.
3. To keep the pennies from tipping over, you must make a spiral. Keep adding pennies until your spiral tower collapses!
4. How many pennies did you use in each tower? Did your spiral tower have more than your straight tower?

• • •

PENNERGY

What you need:
    Ten pennies

What you do:
1. On a flat surface, put nine pennies in a row. Each penny must touch the one next to it. Hold the tenth penny about six inches away from the end of the row. Give it a swift push so that it slides across the table.

Fun with Money

What happened? You gave your energy to the sliding penny. The sliding penny hit the first in the row. The slider stopped. But, the first penny in the row picked up energy from the slider. The energy moved from the first penny to the second penny. The third picks up energy from the second penny and moves it to the fourth. The last penny, having nothing on the other side of it, moves away from the row. This is known as transference of energy.

Who knew you could carry a science experiment right in your pocket!

• • •

SWELL WATER

What you need:
A clear glass
Water
Pennies
A plate or something to set the glass on that will catch the water

What you do:
1. Fill the glass with water to the very top. Put the glass on the plate.
2. Hold a penny close to the edge of the glass and let it gently fall into the water. The water level will rise.
3. Keep adding pennies in the same way. The water level will appear to rise over the top of the glass. If you look closely, you can see the water swell up and over the top without spilling.
4. How many pennies can you add before the water spills?

What happened? You saw a demonstration of surface tension. Water molecules on the surface of the water attract each other so strongly they seem to form a sheet preventing the water from spilling. As you add more pennies, the strain becomes too great, and the surface tension is broken. The water spills.

Variation: Put one penny on a flat surface. With a medicine dropper, slowly place drops of water onto the coin. How many drops do you think you can place on the coin before the water spills off?

"Mint" Your Own Coins

You can make "coins" to use as gifts. Give these tokens as a promise of work to be done, or give them to someone you love to be exchanged for hugs!

What you need:
    One batch salt dough (recipe below)
    Small rubber stamps (simple designs work best), sealing wax stamps, or decorative items you may find around the house that could be used to stamp an impression—for example, a pressed glass vase.
    Pin or an unbent paper clip
    Paint (silver, gold, or copper to make them look like real coins)

Salt dough recipe
What you need:
    1 cup table salt
    1 tablespoon cooking oil
    1¼ cup water
    2 cups flour

What you do:
    In a large mixing bowl, mix salt, oil, and water. Add the flour—a little at a time. Mix well after each addition. *Knead** the dough until smooth. If the dough is too dry, add a small amount of water. If the dough is too sticky, add a sprinkling of flour.
    The dough should be stored in the refrigerator if not used right away.

What you do:
    Work on a smooth surface—a piece of waxed paper is recommended, but you can use a dinner plate just as well.

1. Break off a small bit of salt dough and roll into a ball (marble-sized is good).
2. Press the rubber stamp or decorative item into the ball to flatten it and leave it with a decorated surface.
3. On the back of the coin use the pin or a bent paper clip to put a value on it, or personalize it with your name. The choice of a value is up to you to decide. If you are going to use the coins as a token of work to be done, you can write "one hour." Wouldn't a neighbor love to receive several of these that could be exchanged for babysitting or yard work! You could add milling to the edges. The good thing about making a coin of salt dough is that if you don't like it, you can roll it into a ball and start again!
4. When you have finished making the coins, let them air dry for several days. If you are in a hurry, they can be put on aluminum foil or a baking sheet and placed in an oven at 250 degrees. Bake for several hours until the coins have hardened. Remember to get adult assistance when using the oven.
5. Paint one side of the coin, let dry, then paint the other.

    Optional: Cut a large circle out of a net onion bag, or a scrap of fabric. Put the coins in the middle and gather up the edges. Use a piece of string to tie your coins into a little pouch for gift giving!

Knead means to mix, pat, and squeeze it with your hands. This can be messy, but it's fun!

Chapter 9
Investing

Okay, you earned some money, or you've been given a nice gift of green. Some of it you've spent. Now the money that's left you need to save. You could put it in your wallet, your piggy bank, or take it to a bank and put it to work in a savings account or a CD. But, did you realize that the money you keep in a savings account, even though it is drawing interest, may not be worth as much next year? How can that be? Inflation!

INFLATION

Inflation is a steady increase in prices for goods and services. It results in a decrease in the buying power of money.

What causes inflation? In some cases, it comes from too much money! When people have more money than they need to provide the basics for their families, then they look to buy extras. For example, we would consider telephone service a basic, but a fax machine would be an extra.

It is against the law to reproduce U.S. paper money unless you make it one-fourth smaller or one and a half times larger.

When people want to buy these extras, demand is up. If there are not enough goods to meet the demand, then prices rise. This is known as the law of supply and demand. (If there

What We Buy

The Consumer Price Index (CPI) is based on the spending habits of 4,800 families. Each month the government checks the prices of approximately ninety thousand goods and services typically used by the sample families. When the prices are compared to the prior month's prices, the CPI may have gone up.

You can see how inflation has affected the purchasing power of money in your lifetime. Go to the Web site at *http://woodrow.mpls.frb.fed.us/economy/calc/cpihome.html*.

Type in the year you were born. Then type in the current year. Goods that cost $1 when you were born will be adjusted for today's rate of inflation. Try putting in your parents' years of birth, and see how the buying power of money has changed for them!

are too many goods, and demand is low, then prices go down!)

When prices go up people need to earn more money to pay for goods and services. Wages go up.

In order to cover the costs of increased wages, manu-facturers must raise the prices of their goods. Prices and wages continue to rise steadily.

Inflation can also occur when a country goes to war and goods are scarce.

You can figure out how long it would be before your money is worth half of its present value. Apply the "Rule of 72" we discussed in Chapter 4. The rate of inflation for 1998 was approximately 1.6 percent. If you were to divide 72 by 1.6, you'd come up with 45. If you put your money under the mattress in 1998 and left it there, 45 years later, that money could buy only half of what it could buy in 1998!

How can you stay ahead of inflation? By investing—that is, putting your money into stocks, mutual funds, bonds, real estate, art, or collectibles, and so on, with the expectation that they will increase in value at a rate higher than the rate of inflation. (And the hope that you can sell them and make lots of money!)

In one study of nearly two hundred years of stock market activity, it was found that the average yearly return (or increase in value) for stocks was 9.5 percent. That is not to say that every stock can earn you 9.5 percent, but it is an average, so some stocks earn more and some a lot less! But in any case, if inflation is at 4 percent per year, you come out ahead if you invest in stocks.

FUN FACT

You've heard the term "Wall Street," but did you know that Wall Street is a real place? When the Dutch settled the island of Manhattan (the area we know as New York City) in the 1600s, a portion of the lower tip of the island was walled off with mud and sticks. The wall was built to keep the settlers' cows from wandering away and also as protection. The path along the wall became Wall Street.

Wall Street was close to the docks on the Hudson and East Rivers, and this location led to its becoming a thriving commercial center. At first, commodities such as furs and tobacco were traded, then trading expanded to include real estate, bonds, and other investments.

New York City's wealth and importance continued to grow. During a brief period right after the Revolutionary War (the war ended in 1783), it was the capital of the new United States. George Washington was inaugurated as president at Federal Hall located on Wall Street. The first session of Congress also met at Federal Hall, and one of its first actions was to issue bonds to raise money to pay off the debts of the Revolution. From that time to now, Wall Street has traded in stocks and bonds, and it is now known as the financial capital of the world!

ARE YOU THE INVESTING TYPE?

Are you the type of kid who can be an investor? There are several things you must think about before seriously considering investing.

Examine your own personality. Do you find the idea of buying stock in a new company that may (or may not) come up with the next big electronics miracle exciting? You could make some real money! But, what if the company you invest in fails, and you lose your money? Would you be very upset?

How much money can you invest? Based on your income, from an allowance, gifts, babysitting, and so on, if you can set aside even $100 a year, it might be worth it to you to invest this money.

What are your goals? Do you want to buy Christmas presents for your friends and family? Then investing is not the way to go. To see the results of your investments, you must be willing to be patient and wait. If you are planning on going to college in another eight years, then investing your $100 a year may be something for you and your parents to consider. You wouldn't be able to pay for your whole college education, but you just might be able to cover the cost of your books or set up an account for spending money while you're in college.

Many kids don't realize the amount of time and effort that goes into investing. You "earn" your money by "taking on the job" of investing. Overnight success is rare. If you're looking to get rich quick, forget it. One of the keys to investing is patience! Think five years or more!

> "Money can't buy friends, but you can get a better class of enemy."
> —*Spike Mulligan*

Also, you must remember that in investing you are tying up your money. If you want your money where you can get at it easily, then perhaps a savings account is the best for you.

STOCKS

A stock is a share in a business. Here are some things you should know about stocks:

- When a new company feels a need to expand, it may not have the money to do so. A decision is made to "go public." By going public, a company decides to sell shares (stock) in its business. The people in charge of the business now have to report to the shareholders, who each "own" a tiny part of the company.
- The "initial public offering" (IPO) is the first time stock is sold by that company. Investment bankers buy up the stock and then are responsible for selling it. It is interesting to note that this is the only time the company makes money from sale of its stock. From this point on, the buying and selling of stock is in the hands of the investment bank and brokers.
- The shares of stock are sold to investors. Investors come from all walks of life. They may also include groups other than individuals—for example, institutions.
- Each shareholder may vote at an annual meeting to elect directors of the business.
- Each share has an equal vote, but the more shares a person owns, the greater the number of votes the person has.
- Businesses that make a profit pay dividends to their stockholders. Those companies that make high divi-

FUN FACT

Private

Some companies are privately held. That is, they are owned by individuals. No public offering has been made, so you will not find them in the stock listings.

Go to the public library and look up a company in a reference book such as *Hoover's Handbook of American Business* or *Value Line Investment Survey*. Ask the reference librarian to show you other resources.

Online there are numerous sites listing company information and current market activity. The advantage to doing your research online is that the information is updated daily!

dend payments to their stockholders every year are called "income stocks." People buy income stocks so that they can depend on a steady income from their shares.

- Some companies may use profits to make improvements to the business. They may not pay dividends, or if they do, they are small. The stock for these companies is called "growth stock." Growth stocks are expected to grow in value because the company has improved or expanded and can go on to make more money.

- Stocks are traded on exchanges, special places where stocks are bought and sold. The New York Stock Exchange (NYSE), and the American Stock Exchange (AMEX) are the primary exchanges in the United States. The National Association of Securities Dealers Automatic Quotation System (Nasdaq) sells stocks not "listed" with an exchange. These are called "Over the Counter" (OTC).

- A person who buys and sells stocks for a client is called a **broker.**

THE INVESTING GAME

A good way to explore the world of the stock market is to make your first investment with imaginary money! Give yourself $1,000 (or more, it's not real!) and think about a product you are interested in. It can be your favorite candy bar, soda, running shoes, or computer software.

Find out who makes the product. For example, let's say you just had Rice•Krispies for breakfast. Look at the box to find that Kellogg Company makes the cereal.

Go to the library and look for the *Wall Street Journal*. You can also go to the financial section of a large newspaper to find the stock or stocks you are considering. (Or online you can try *www.amex.com*.)

You'll find several pages of letters and numbers! Don't be scared away! Look for a listing with a heading for the NYSE.

Now let's see how we "read" a stock listing:

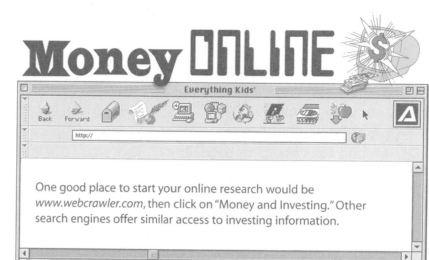

One good place to start your online research would be *www.webcrawler.com*, then click on "Money and Investing." Other search engines offer similar access to investing information.

1. *52 Weeks* is a year. The *Hi* and *Lo* are the highest and lowest prices the stocks have been traded for over the past year. The numbers may be given in fractions, 1/8 = 12 1/2 cents, 1/4 = 25 cents, 3/8 = 37 1/2 cents, 1/2 = 50 cents, 5/8 = 62 1/2 cents, 3/4 = 75 cents, and 7/8 = 87 1/2 cents.

2. *The Stock* is the company name. It may be abbreviated to save space.

3. *Sym* is the "ticker" symbol that represents the company. A ticker is an old fashioned way of reporting stock transactions. Symbols and prices were transmitted telegraphically on long skinny pieces of paper called ticker tape. Today, this information is transmitted electronically through computers and networks. For Kellogg Company the symbol is K.

4. *Yld* stands for "yield"—the cash you'd expect to get from your investment in this particular stock.

5. *Div* is the estimated dividend to be paid per share.

6. *%* is what percentage of your investment you will receive in dividends.

FUN FACT

Liquid Money

How fast you can turn your investment into cash is known as "liquidity." With a savings account it is easy to get the cash, but with stocks it is a more complicated process. You have to contact your broker to sell the stock for you. Real estate or collectibles are even less liquid. When you need to sell, there may not be anyone willing to buy! Cash in hand is the most liquid of all.

7. *PE* stands for "price-earnings ratio." It refers to the relation between the price of one share, and the per share annual earnings of the company. The P/E = price divided by earnings. A P/E around 15 is about average. It would take fifteen years for the stock to pay for itself if the earnings did not change.
8. *Vol 100s* is how many shares of stock were traded that day. Take the figure listed and multiply by 100. Stock is usually sold in "lots" of 100 called a "round lot." Less than 100 shares is called an odd lot.
9. *Hi* is the highest price for the day. *Lo* is the lowest price for the day. *Close* is the price of the share in its last trade of the day.
10. *Net Chg* is the comparison of the price at the close of the day with the price at the close of the previous day's trading. If the price went down, it is shown by a minus sign (-). If the price went up, it is shown by a plus sign (+). Any listing in **bold** print shows a share that has had a change of 5 percent or more.

NEW YORK STOCK EXCHANGE ISSUES

52-Week High	52-Week Low	Stock	Div	Yld %	P/E	Sales 100s	High	Low	Last	Chg
		A								
24	**14 5/8**	**AAR**	**.34**	**1.9**	**11**	**4024**	**18 1/4**	**16 1/16**	**17 15/16**	**+1 3/8**
34 1/2	20 1/8	▼ABM	.62 f	3.0	12	5169	20 7/8	20	20 3/8	− 1/16
25 13/16	19	ABN Amro	.62 e	2.4		1073	25 5/16	24 3/4	25 5/16	+ 1/16
35 1/4	15 1/2	♣ACE Ltd	.44	2.6	7	x49558	17 1/8	16	16 11/16	+ 1/2
9 1/2	6 5/16	ACMIn	.90 a	14.0	q	11790	6 5/8	6 3/8	6 7/16	− 1/16
7 15/16	6 1/4	ACM Op	.63 a	8.7	q	x1804	7 1/4	6 5/16	7 1/4	+ 15/16
8 3/4	6 3/16	ACM Sc	.90	14.1	q	15575	6 1/2	6 5/16	6 3/8	− 1/16
6 1/4	5 3/8	ACMSp	.54	9.9	q	4324	5 9/16	5 7/16	5 7/16	− 1/16
11 1/2	8 7/16	▼ACMMD	1.35 a	16.1	q	x4729	8 11/16	8 1/4	8 3/8	− 1/8
9 1/4	5 13/16	▼ACM MI	1.02 a	17.4	q	x5548	6 1/8	5 5/8	5 7/8	...
14 1/4	10 1/8	ACMMu	.87	8.2	q	1841	10 11/16	10 1/8	10 5/8	+ 3/8
32 3/4	**19 7/8**	**ACNiels**	...	...	**21**	**8803**	**24 7/8**	**21 3/4**	**24 5/8**	**+2 3/16**
16 11/16	**7 1/2**	**♣ACX Tech**	...	...	**7**	**4993**	**10 3/4**	**9 1/2**	**10 11/16**	**+1**
70 7/8	**32 13/16**	**▲♣AES Cp**	...	...	**70**	**24304**	**76 3/8**	**69**	**74 3/4**	**+6 13/16**
56 3/4	39	AFLAC	.30	0.6	22	21472	47 11/16	43 1/2	47 3/16	+2 1/16
14 1/8	6	AGCO	.04	0.3	dd	10395	13 13/16	12 11/16	13 7/16	− 1/8
23 3/8	15 9/16	AGL Res	1.08	6.4	13	4650	17 1/4	16 9/16	17	− 1/16
29 5/8	**13 3/4**	**♣AK Steel**	**.50**	**2.6**	**15**	**26008**	**19 1/16**	**17 1/16**	**18 7/8**	**+1 7/8**
23 1/2	18	♣AMB Pr	1.40	7.0	12	4338	20 1/16	19	19 15/16	+ 5/8
8 1/4	2 5/16	AMF Bowl	...	...	dd	5597	3 1/8	2 5/8	3 1/8	+ 5/16
79 3/4	39 1/2	AMFM	...	...	dd	26903	78 11/16	76 5/16	78 1/4	+ 1/4
23	18 7/8	♣AMLI Rs	1.84 f	9.1	12	1432	20 3/8	19 3/4	20 3/16	+ 7/16
75 7/16	52 9/16	AMR	...	...	11	20673	68 1/16	63 11/16	67	+ 3/16
24 5/8	20 1/2	▼AMR Cp 39	1.97	9.6		1770	20 7/8	19 9/16	20 9/16	− 1/4
7 1/8	2 3/8	APT Sat	...	...		3040	5	4 1/8	4 5/8	+ 5/16
24	14 15/16	ASA Ltd	.60	3.2	q	3198	19 1/4	18 11/16	18 15/16	− 1/16

52-Week High	52-Week Low	Stock	Div	Yld %	P/E	Sales 100s	High	Lo
91 13/16	56 5/16	Alltel	1.22	1.5	36	35680	83 7/16	76
34	19 7/16	♣Alltrista	...	...	5	400	23 9/16	21
43 3/8	**24 9/16**	**♣Alpharma**	**.18**	**0.6**	**24**	**4902**	**30 7/8**	**27**
18 5/8	**9 3/8**	**AlpineGr**	...	...	**4**	**2440**	**12 7/8**	**11**
35 9/16	22 1/2	Alstom	...	...		178	34	33
55 3/4	**26**	**Alza**	...	...	**33**	**97812**	**34 15/16**	**31**
63	44 11/16	♣AmbacF	.44	0.8	13	9233	53	50
25 3/4	19 3/4	▼AmbacF98	1.77	8.6		1947	20 1/2	19
22	**12 3/8**	**♣Amcast**	**.56**	**3.4**	**14**	**4666**	**17**	**14**
17 7/8	8 1/4	AMCOL	.28	1.7	15	1638	16 1/4	15
37 15/16	13 1/2	Amdocs	...	...	70	12655	35 7/16	33
35	20 3/16	AmdocsTr	1.51	4.7		1225	32 1/2	31
27 11/16	18 1/4	AmrUs01	2.21	9.7		1959	23 7/8	22
66 5/16	43 3/4	AmHes	.60	1.1	dd	11453	57 1/2	54
42 15/16	32	Ameren	2.54	7.8	11	19213	33 3/8	32
5 13/16	4	AmrFMI	.56 f	12.3	6	x554	4 7/8	4
95 13/16	32 1/2	AmOnline s	...	...	cc	824951	81 1/2	74
24 1/8	16	AmWest	...	...	7	9025	21 1/4	20
25	15 5/8	AAnnuity	.10	0.6	11	197	18	17
17 3/8	11 5/8	▼AmAxle n	...	...		1133	12 7/16	11
23 5/8	10 1/4	ABusnP	.66	5.6	16	1235	11 11/16	10
48 3/16	30 9/16	♣AEP	2.40	7.5	13	14035	32 13/16	32
168 7/8	94 7/8	AmExp	.90	0.5	32	42064	168	158
43 5/8	24 1/2	AFnclGp	1.00	3.8	18	2718	27 1/4	25
82 3/16	61 7/8	♣AGenCp	1.60	2.1	22	14329	76 1/4	71
44 5/16	22	AGreet	.80	3.4	17	10620	25 1/4	23
70 1/4	38 1/2	▼AHomeP	.92 f	2.3	dd	221155	41 3/16	36
15	9 9/16	♣AIndPrp	.80	6.5	cc	522	12 15/16	11

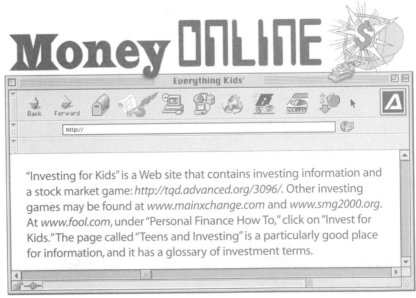

Money ONLINE

Everything Kids'

Back Forward

http://

"Investing for Kids" is a Web site that contains investing information and a stock market game: *http://tqd.advanced.org/3096/*. Other investing games may be found at *www.mainxchange.com* and *www.smg2000.org*. At *www.fool.com*, under "Personal Finance How To," click on "Invest for Kids." The page called "Teens and Investing" is a particularly good place for information, and it has a glossary of investment terms.

Find your stock by looking down the alphabetical listing. Examine each of the numbers. Is the dividend high or low? Is there a dividend at all? Compare the 52-week high/low figures. If there's a big difference, why do you think that is?

Go to the public library and look up your company in a reference book such as *Hoover's Handbook of American Business* or *Value Line Investment Survey*. Ask the reference librarian to show you other resources.

Online there are numerous sites listing company information and current market activity. The advantage to doing your research online is that the information is updated daily!

Decide if the stock you've investigated would be a good choice for you. If so, then use the "close" price in today's paper and figure out how many shares you could buy with $1000. You've begun the "investing game."

Set a date in the future, perhaps six months, when you will finish tracking your stock. Over the six months, look at the stock listings. This doesn't have to be done daily, once a week would be good. You might want to graph your stock's price on a weekly basis.

At the six-month point, take the close price that day and multiply it by the number of shares you bought with your original $1000. How did you do? Did you make money? If so, what is the percentage of increase? (Divide the present value of your stock by the amount you started with, $1,000. For example, your stock is now worth $1,150. If you divide 1150 by 1000, you will get 1.15. What that figure means is a 15 percent increase!)

Direct Stock Purchase

There is a way to invest in the stock market without going through a broker. It's called a Direct Purchase Program. An investor directly contacts a company to purchase stock. A similar program called a Dividend Reinvestment Plan (DRIP) allows shareholders to automatically reinvest dividends in more stock. Not all companies have this option available. The "Kidstock" Web site at *www.kidstock.com* has information about direct purchase programs. A good place for adults to read more about DRIPs is in Charles B. Carlson's *Buying Stocks without a Broker* (McGraw-Hill, 1996).

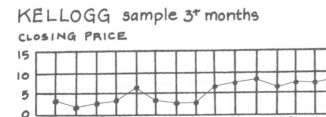

KELLOGG sample 3+ months
CLOSING PRICE

WORDS to KNOW

Portfolio—all of your investments.

Diversification—to have a number of different types of investments. It is a way to reduce risk. Say for instance, you had all your money tied up in computer stocks. One day everyone decides to throw away their computers and go back to using pencil and paper. The price of computer stocks would go way down, and you would lose your money. Now say you had a diversified portfolio with some computer stock, some cat food company stock, some office supply store stock, and some movie company stock. When the market for computers died, you would lose only some of your money because you had invested in other types of stock. The price of your office supply store stock would go up because of the renewed interest in paper and pencils!

If you feel comfortable with the results of your investing game, then perhaps you'd like to ask your parents if you could try investing with real money. By law, you are not able to invest on your own if you are not of legal age. The definition of legal age varies from state to state. Your parents would have to set up a "custodial" or "guardian" account for you. Or maybe your parents invest in the stock market themselves and they could show you how some of their investments have done and what they use to help them make decisions.

How do you go about investing with real money? You could find a broker, someone who does the buying and selling for you. There are basically two types of brokers—the full-service broker who not only trades stocks for you, but also provides you with investment advice; and the discount broker who merely buys and sells stock that you tell him or her to. The advantage to the discount broker is that the fees for the service are less than for a full-service broker. If you are new to investing, or can't take the time to do your own research, then it may be worth it to pay the extra for the advice of a professional.

If your parents or relatives want to purchase stock for you, let them know about the Uniform Gift to Minors Act (UGMA) and the Uniform Transfer to Minors Act (UTMA). These acts allow adults to have control over the gifts or transfers of money, stock, real estate, and so on, to children under legal age, or in the case of UTMA, children up to 25 years of age. There are tax advantages to setting up this kind of account. To find out more, your parents can order IRS publication 929, "Tax Rules for Children and Dependents," by calling 1-800-TAX-FORM.

What do you call a rabbit who makes counterfeit bills?

A funny money bunny.

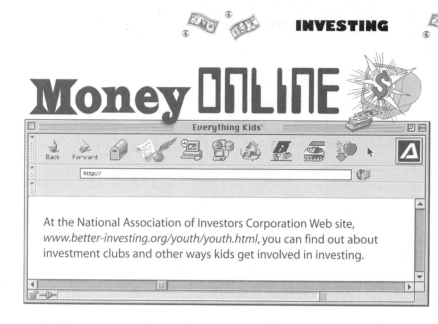

Money ONLINE

Everything Kids'

http://

At the National Association of Investors Corporation Web site, *www.better-investing.org/youth/youth.html*, you can find out about investment clubs and other ways kids get involved in investing.

What do you call a rabbit who works in a bank?

A money bunny.

MUTUAL FUNDS

Mutual Fund investing is perfect for the investor who has neither the time nor the desire to research individual companies, wants **diversification**, and doesn't have a lot of money.

What is a mutual fund? A mutual fund is a group of people (investors) pooling their money to invest in a group of stocks, bonds, and other securities.

A mutual fund is controlled by a person known as a "fund manager." The fund manager, through his or her knowledge and experience, selects a number of different securities for the fund. Mutual funds are available through brokerage houses and investment companies.

Mutual funds come in the following varieties:

- *Stock funds*—which own stock in companies. Like stocks, mutual funds can be defined as growth or income investments.
- *Bond funds*—which own a number of different bonds, or specialize in one type of bond.

FUN FACT

The Trading Floor

Stock exchanges operate with auction-type trading—that is, a stock is sold to the highest bidder. The exchange does not set prices, they are determined by supply and demand. Supply and demand means that if the supply of something, say a stock, is low, and the number of people who want it is high, then the price goes up because people are willing to pay more to get what they want. If the supply is great, then people are less willing to buy, so the price goes down. For a look at how the actual trading works at a stock exchange, visit *www.nyse.com/floor/floor.html*.

- *Money market funds*—which own short-term investments such as CDs.
- *Balanced funds*—which own both stocks and bonds.
- *Real estate investment trust (REIT)*—buys real estate (buildings).
- Other funds invest in gold or foreign stocks and bonds.

Diversification and professional management are the main advantages to mutual funds. For instance, a stock fund will invest in the stocks of a variety of different industries. Over a period of time, some stock may go down, others may go up. But, it is hoped that the fund has more ups so that the total value of your investment grows over time!

Some mutual funds allow you to invest with smaller amounts of money than would be required by a brokerage house for investing in stocks. There are even some plans where you can invest a fixed amount each month.

The disadvantage to mutual funds is that the return on your investment may not be as high as the return on the stock market. Remember the 9.5 percent average yearly return on stocks? Typically, a mutual fund does not earn as much.

In order to make money, a fund must charge fees for its fund management. It may also charge fees for investing your money. These fees are referred to as "load." Some funds are "no-load," meaning they have no commissions—but don't be misled into thinking "no-load" means no money paid. You still must pay the management fees.

Funds offer an investor a "prospectus." A prospectus is a written statement of the fund's objectives—what it hopes to do. It also tells you what the fund's performance history is, what its fees are, special features, the minimum required to invest in the fund, and the level of risk. For example, growth stock mutual funds are riskier than income stock funds. Before investing in any mutual fund, a person should read the

FUN FACT

There are even mutual funds that invest in mutual funds! These are called "megafunds."

prospectus carefully. The investor can also do a little research by going to the library and looking at the *Morningstar Mutual Funds*, a weekly rating of mutual funds.

Like the stock market, mutual funds are listed in the financial pages of newspapers. Here's how to "read" them:

1. The name of the company managing the fund is listed alphabetically. Under each family name, is the type of mutual fund or funds offered.
2. *NAV* is the net asset value. It is the dollar value of one share of the fund. If you were to sell the share back to the company, this would be the price you would get.
3. *Dly % Ret.* Ret is "return." The figure stand for the percentage difference between today's NAV and yesterday's.
4. *YTD % Ret* is the percentage change for the year from January 1 through today. Some mutual fund listings will also include 3-year and 5-year figures.

This brief examination of stocks and mutual funds is only a beginning look at the investment opportunities kids can look forward to. If you are interested in finding out more, you're in luck. Hundreds of books have been written about investing! Just go to your local library or bookstore and prepare to be overwhelmed with the amount of information available to you. Try *The Everything Investing Book* by Rich Mintzer (Adams Media Corp., 1999) for a start.

MUTUAL FUNDS

Fund Family Fund Name	Type	Rating	NAV	Wkly. % Ret.	YTD % Ret.	1-Yr. % Ret.	3-Mo. % Ret.
AAL A (800) 553-6319							
Balanced m	DH	NA	12.60	...	+11.0	+11.0	+ 7.7
Bond m	CI	3/3	9.41	...	− 1.6	− 1.6	− 0.1
CapGrow m	LB	4/5	39.60	− 0.1	+22.6	+22.6	+15.0
EqInc m	LV	3/3	14.29	+ 1.1	+ 4.1	+ 4.1	+ 4.5
HiYld m	HY	NA	7.88	+ 0.1	− 3.7	− 3.7	+ 0.3
Intl m	FS	3/3	14.94	+ 2.6	+39.7	+39.7	+23.4
MidCap m	MG	2/2	15.63	+ 2.1	+18.3	+18.3	+16.3
MuniBond m	ML	1/2	10.37	− 0.1	− 5.6	− 5.6	− 1.9
SmCapStk m	SG	1/2	13.33	+ 3.6	+13.2	+13.2	+19.1
AALCapGrB (800) 553-6319							
AALCapGrB m	LB	NA	38.76	− 0.1	+21.3	+21.3	+14.7
AARP Investment (800) 322-2282							
BalStkBd	DH	3/2	19.52	+ 0.3	+ 2.9	+ 2.9	+ 3.8
Bdforinc	CI	NA	13.97	− 0.1	− 0.9	− 0.9	+ 0.2
CapGrow	LB	5/5	72.55	+ 1.3	+35.4	+35.4	+24.5
DivrGrow	DH	NA	18.90	+ 1.1	+12.6	+12.6	+10.5
DivrIncGr	DH	NA	15.83	+ 0.3	+ 5.0	+ 5.0	+ 4.5
GNMAUSTrs	GS	4/3	14.40	...	+ 0.5	+ 0.5	+ 0.1
GloGrow	WS	3/3	21.43	+ 2.9	+22.1	+22.1	+15.8
GrowInc	LV	3/3	49.99	+ 0.3	+ 7.4	+ 7.4	+ 6.6
HiQShTmBd	CS	4/NA	15.67	+ 0.1	+ 2.1	+ 2.1	+ 1.0
InsTaxFBd	ML	4/4	17.43	+ 0.2	− 2.1	− 2.1	− 0.4
IntlGrInc	FS	NA	23.70	+ 4.3	+35.7	+35.7	+29.0
SmCpStk	SV	NA	17.99	+ 3.8	− 3.5	− 3.5	+ 0.7
USStkIdx	LB	NA	27.91	+ 1.0	+22.0	+22.0	+15.0
ABN AMRO (800) 443-4725							
AsiaTigCm	PJ	1/3	10.92	+ 1.8	+62.3	+62.3	+26.7
BalComm	DH	3/3	11.96	+ 0.5	+10.5	+10.5	+ 8.1
FixInComm	CI	3/3	9.57	...	− 2.1	− 2.1	− 0.6
GrowComm	LG	3/2	17.44	+ 0.2	+12.8	+12.8	+18.0

"Nothing but money is sweeter than honey." —*Benjamin Franklin*

COLLECTIBLES

Do you have a Beanie Baby? Or maybe on your shelf in your room you keep a couple of metal lunchboxes your dad had as a kid. Surely you've seen a baseball card or at least chewed

FUN FACT

In 1955, twenty-four thousand pennies were mistakenly released to the public. The lettering and the date on the face of these pennies were accidentally stamped twice so there is a double image! The penny quickly became a hot collector's item and is known as the "1955 Double Die Cent." Within three years the price for a Double Die Cent was up to $7.50. In five years time it had jumped to $60.00. To purchase a 1955 Double Die Cent today you'll have to dish out close to $1,000!

Don't Wash Those Coins

A shiny penny is not necessarily a valuable penny if you've scoured it to get the shine. Coin collectors will tell you that in most cases if you clean coins you will reduce their numismatic value. Even using a soft cloth to wipe the coins can cause small scratches! If you find a coin that has dirt or some other sticky substance on it, you could try to remove it by soaking the coin in olive oil for several days. Drain off the olive oil, soak in soap and water to remove the oil, then rinse the coin and let dry.

some gum from one! These are collectibles. Collectibles are things that have value to collectors. A collection of dust bunnies from under your bed wouldn't be collectibles, but a collection of comic books would.

Collectibles are an investment opportunity kids sometimes think about. Everyone dreams about finding an old coin that is worth thousands! Unfortunately, the risk involved does not make collectibles investment a good choice for kids. But, collecting can be fun, and if your collection increases in value over the years, won't that be great?

If your collection has potential value, then it is important for you to learn all you can about the collection and how to care for it. As an example, let's look at coin collecting.

Are all coins collectable? Absolutely! If you find them beautiful or interesting, then that's reason enough for you to collect them. But, it is only the valuable ones that can be bought and sold for investment purposes.

What gives collectible coins their value? Rarity and condition. By rarity we mean how difficult is it to find another coin just like it. If only a few examples of a particular coin are known to exist, then their rarity makes them valuable.

Condition is the shape the coin is in. The best condition is known as "mint" condition. That is, the coin is as good as the day it came from the mint. The more worn a coin becomes, the poorer its condition and the less it is worth. But, a coin in poor condition could still have value if it is rare!

Abe's Pocket Change

Think about this—you buy an 1860 U.S. penny. What if this coin had been in the pocket of Abraham Lincoln? Is there anyone who can tell you it never happened? No! That's part of the attraction of coin collecting—you never know who could have owned it before you!

How do you find the value of a coin?

1. Check a price guide such as the *Guide to U.S. Coins, Prices and Value Trends* by the editors of *Coin World*.
2. Read coin collecting magazines such as *Coin Prices* and *Coins*.
3. Talk to coin dealers and numismatists (coin experts).
4. Go to coin shows, and join coin collectors' organizations.

Does it sound like a lot of work? It is, but if you've read this far in the Investing chapter, then you know that investing takes work.

Where can you find collectible coins? You can find them at coin shops and coin shows, through mail order, or on-line. The U.S. Mint has special "proof sets" of coins that you can buy directly from the mint.

You can also check with your parents and grandparents to see if they have any old coins. If they do, ask if you could research them. Look them up in price guides and find out their history. If you're lucky, you'll find something of value.

What kinds of coins should you collect? I'd suggest collecting the things that interest you. Silver dollars, or minting errors, or perhaps you'd like to collect one dime from every year they were minted. If you'd like to collect foreign coins, you could specialize in coins that have ships on them, or ones that have trees. The choice is up to you.

Did I mention that investing in coins, like investing in the stock market or putting your money in CDs, takes time and patience? It may take you years to collect a dime from every year, but think of all the fun you'll have doing it. It's the thrill of the hunt! In 1804 there were only 8,265 dimes minted. How many of these do you think survived over the nearly two hundred years since they were minted? Imagine adding one of

Coin collecting has a long history. *The Virtuoso's Companion and Coin Collector's Guide*, a British guidebook, was published in 1795!

FUN FACT

Dig for Treasure

A more unusual source of collectible coins is the earth beneath your feet! Collectors equipped with metal detectors find not only coins, but jewelry and other objects of value. *The New Successful Coin Hunting* by Charles Garrett (Ram Books, 1997) is full of stories of found "treasure."

Money ONLINE

Everything Kids'

http://

Did you know that stories of pirate treasure may be real? The Web site *www.coinworld.com/reading/statetreasures1.html* reveals lost "treasure" waiting to be found. Look for your state's treasure listing and get out your metal detector!

FUN FACT

American Numismatic Association

The largest coin collectors' organization in the world is the American Numismatic Association (ANA). The ANA is one of the few organizations to have been chartered by Congress! For information about the group visit their Web site at *www.money.org*, or write to the American Numismatic Association, 818 North Cascade Avenue, Colorado Springs, Colorado 80903-3279. The ANA has a special junior membership rate of $11 per year. For an application call 1-800-367-9723

the 1804s to your collection. You may have to wait until you grow up and get a job before you can afford one!

Why not start your collection by saving the new fifty states quarters? Or, find one of those Susan B. Anthony dollars that seem to have disappeared. Start small, you won't make a million overnight!

But maybe someday you will make a million. On August 30, 1999, a silver dollar minted in 1804, one of only fifteen known pieces, went on the auction block and sold for a record-breaking $4.14 million! You read that right! $4.14 million!

Another of these 1804 dollars had sold in 1997 for $1.815 million. Imagine if you bought a silver dollar at $1.815 million and turned around and sold it two years later for $4.14 million! You would have more than doubled your investment! That sure beats the stock market!

"If you have money, you are wise and good looking and can sing well too."
—*Yiddish proverb*

Fun with Money

Mancala

Here's a simple game that's been around for thousands of years. It's played all over the African continent and in other locations throughout the world.

Mancala can be played very simply just by scooping out small holes in the dirt, but you'll stay much cleaner if you make your own board!

What you need:

Two empty twelve-compartment egg cartons
Glue (a glue gun or rubber cement works best for this project)
Crayons, markers, or paint to decorate (optional)
Forty-eight pennies

What you do:

1. Cut off the top of the egg carton and throw it away. Trim the edges of the bottom compartment piece. Have fun decorating it if you want.

2. Cut two individual egg holders from the second egg carton. Glue the two egg holders to the sides of the egg compartment as shown. Your mancala board is now ready.

How to play:

This game is played with 2 people. The board is placed between the players so that each person has a six-compartment side. The individual holder to the right of each player is known as the "kalaha."

To set up, each player takes twenty-four pennies and puts four into each of the six small compartments. The kalahas are empty at the start. You must start each turn from one of the compartments on your side of the board.

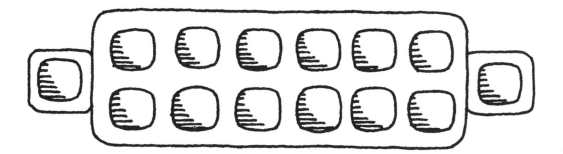

Fun with Money

The object of the game is to end up with the most coins in your kalaha.

Decide who will go first. How? Why, toss a coin, of course!

1. Player 1 takes all the coins from any one of the compartments on his or her side. Moving to the right, Player 1 places one penny in each bin, even the kalaha, and continues around to Player 2's compartments if necessary.

2. If Player 1's last penny ends up in the kalaha, he or she goes again. If the last penny lands anywhere else, Player 2 gets to go.

3. Continue playing. Eventually a player will come to his or her opponent's kalaha. An opponent's kalaha gets skipped.

4. If a player's last piece is dropped into an empty compartment on his or her side of the board, then he or she gets to take all the pennies in the compartment directly opposite. This is a "capture." The captured pennies are placed in the capturer's kalaha and his or her turn is finished.

5. The game ends when all the compartments on any one side are empty. The player whose side still has pennies takes those pennies and adds them to his or her kalaha.

6. Each player counts the number of pennies in his or her kalaha. The one with the most wins.

This game is deceptively easy. After a while you will figure out strategies, then don't be surprised if you and a friend find yourselves playing for hours!

Mancala comes from an Arabic word meaning, "to transfer."

WORD origin

FUN FACT

Mancala is known by other names depending on where it's played. In Vietnam, it's called *Rambool*. In South Africa, the name is *Ohoro*.

$ $ $

In India, Maharajahs supposedly played this game with rubies and other precious gems!

Conclusion

A FEW THOUGHTS ABOUT MONEY

I hope you know a little more about money now than when you started! Although I've tried to include EVERYTHING, there is too much to fit into one book! So, if you're interested in learning more, take a look at some of the resources listed in the section that follows.

If you're still looking for the answer to Chelsea D.'s question, "How do I make a lot of money fast?" I'm afraid you won't find it! As far as I can tell, there is no way to make money fast. As we saw in the chapters on earning and investing, the key to making money is to plan, work hard, and be patient!

Good luck!

Resources

Note: every effort was made to include print resources that are currently available, and all Web sites listed were active as of September 1999. Please be aware that URLs and Web site content often change, and materials frequently go out of print.

BOOKS FOR KIDS

Adelstein, Amy. *Money (Money and Me)*. Rourke Book Co., 1997.

Berg, Adriane G. *The Totally Awesome Money Book for Kids (And Their Parents)*. Newmarket Press, 1993.

Cribb, Joe. *Money (Eyewitness Books)*. Alfred A. Knopf, 1990.

Godfrey, Neale S. *Neale S. Godfrey's Ultimate Kids' Money Book*. Simon & Schuster Books for Young Readers, 1998.

Grimshaw, Caroline. *Money*. World Book, Inc., 1997.

Otfinoski, Steve. *The Kids' Guide to Money: Earning It, Spending It, Growing It, Sharing It*. Scholastic Inc., 1996.

Moose, Christina J. *Budgeting (Money and Me)*. Rourke Book Co., 1997.

Moose, Christina J. *Debt (Money and Me)*. Rourke Book Co., 1997.

Parker, Nancy Winslow. *Money, Money, Money: The Meaning of Art and Symbols on United States Paper Currency*. Harper Collins Children's Books, 1995.

Sobczak, Ray. *Financial Markets (Money and Me)*. Rourke Book Co., 1997.

BOOKS FOR ADULTS

Bamford, Janet, et al. *The Consumer Reports Money Book: How to Get It, Save It, and Spend It Wisely*, 3rd edition. Consumer Union of United States, Inc. 1997.

Mintzer, Rich, with Annette Racond. *The Everything Investing Book*. Adams Media Corporation, 1999.

Mintzer, Rich, with Kathi Mintzer. *The Everything Money Book*. Adams Media Corporation, 1999.

Pearl, Jayne A. *Kids and Money: Giving Them the Savvy to Succeed Financially*. Bloomberg Press, 1999.

Weatherford, Jack. *The History of Money: From Sandstone to Cyberspace*. Three Rivers Press, 1998.

Wiegold, C. Frederic. *The Wall Street Lifetime Guide to Money: Everything You Need to Know About Managing Your Finances—For Every Stage of Life*. Hyperion, 1997.

Williams, Jonathan, ed. *Money: A History*. St. Martin's Press, 1997.

MAGAZINES FOR KIDS

Kids' Wall Street News: The News and Financial Publication for Young Adults. P.O. Box 1207, Rancho Santa Fe, CA 92067, $19.95 (6 issues/yr.), *www.kwsnews.com*

Young Money: Teens Earn It, Invest It, Spend It. P. O. Box 637, Loveland, OH 45140, $14.95 (6 issues/yr.), *www.youngmoney.com*.

Zillions. P. O. Box 54861, Boulder, CO 80322-4061, $16.00 (6 issues/yr.), *www.zillionsedcenter.org/*.

The "Z-Team" is one hundred kids around the country who test products and do projects for *Zillions*. Kids who are interested in being on the "Z-Team" should look at the March/April issue each year for the essay contest used to select the team members. One thousand runners-up in the contest can become members of the "Q-Team," kids who fill out questionnaires for the magazine.

WEB SITES

American Numismatic Society: *www.amnumsoc.org*

Bureau of Engraving and Printing: *www.moneyfactory.com*

History of Money: *www.ex.ac.uk/~Rdavies/arian/llyfr.html*

Investor Words: *www.investorwords.com*

Kids and Money: *www.investorguide.com/Kids.htm*

Money Museum: *http://www.moneymuseum.com/index_english.html*

Numismatica: *www.limunltd.com/numismatica*
Penny Information Home Page: *www.pennies.org*
National Numismatic Collection:
www.si.edu/organiza/museums/nmah/csr/cadnnc.htm
United States Mint: *www.usmint.gov*
United States Treasury Educational Links: *www.ustreas.gov/*
   education.html

MUSEUMS

The Institute for Monetary and Economic Studies, the Bank of Japan
   Currency Museum
Nihonbashi-Hongokucho, Chuo-ku Tokyo 103 Japan
Phone: 03-3277-3037
www.imes.boj.or.jp/cm/english_htmls/index.htm

Museum of American Financial History
28 Broadway, New York, NY 10004
Phone: (212) 908-4519
www.mafh.org

The Royal Coin Cabinet—National Museum of Monetary History
Box 5428, S-114 84 Stockholm, Sweden
Phone: +46-(0)8-51955300
www.myntkabinettet.se (click on the British flag for the English
   language version)

INDEX